Guide to London's
Contemporary Architecture

Guide to London's Contemporary Architecture

Kenneth Allinson
AADipl RIBA MAPM
and
Victoria Thornton

Butterworth Architecture
An imprint of Butterworth-Heinemann Ltd
Linacre House, Jordan Hill, Oxford OX2 8DP

A member of the Reed Elsevier group

OXFORD   LONDON   BOSTON
MUNICH   NEW DELHI   SINGAPORE   SYDNEY
TOKYO   TORONTO   WELLINGTON

First published 1993

British Library Cataloguing in Publication Data
Allinson, Kenneth
  Guide to London's Contemporary
  Architecture
  I. Title II. Thornton, Victoria
  720.9421
ISBN 0 7506 0782 3

Library of Congress Cataloguing in Publication Data
Allinson, Kenneth
  Guide to London's contemporary architecture/Kenneth Allinson
  and Victoria Thornton
  p.   cm.
  Includes indexes.
  ISBN 0 7506 0782 3
  1. Architecture. Modern – 20th century – England – London –
  Guidebooks. 2. London (England) – Buildings, structures, etc.
  I. Thornton, Victoria. II. Title.
  NA970.T56   1993
  720'.9421'09048–dc20   93–15283
                                                      CIP

Cover photographs by Graham Challifour
Composition by Scribe Design, Gillingham, Kent
Printed and bound in Great Britain

Contents

Preface   vii
Introduction   x
London: significant contemporary
    dialogues   xii

A. The City of London   1
A1. Lloyd's of London   2
A2. Broadgate Complex   4
A3. Alban Gate   6
A4. Bracken House   7
A5. Whitechapel Gallery   8
City directions 1: Post-modernism   9
A6. Fenchurch Street offices   9
A7. Queen Street offices   9
A8. Girozentrale Vienna   10
A9. Cornhill offices   10
A10. Minster Court   10
A11. 85 London Wall   11
A12. Fleet Place   11
City directions 2: Hi-tech   12
A13. Billingsgate Securities Market   12
A14. Insignia House   13
A15. Milton Gate   13

B. Docklands   14
Isle of Dogs and the Royals   16
B1. Heron Quays development   17
B2. Canary Wharf   18
Three housing developments: 20
    B3. Cascades   20
    B4. Ferry Street   20
    B5. Compass Point   21
Two pumping stations: 22
    B6. Stewart Street Pumping Station   23
    B7. Royal Victoria Dock Pumping
        Station   23
B8. Financial Times Printing Works   24
B9. Reuters Technical Services Centre   25
B10. Isle of Dogs Neighbourhood Centre   26
B11. Thames Flood Barrier   27
Wapping and Limehouse   28
B12. Roy Square   29
B13. Shadwell Basin   30
B14. Tobacco Dock   31
B15. La Lumiere   32
Butler's Wharf and Surrey Docks   33
B16. Horselydown development   34
B17. Design Museum   35

Two small office buildings: 36
B18. David Mellor building   36
B19. Saffron Wharf   36
Two by CZWG: 37
B20. The Circle   37
B21. China Wharf   37
B22. Hays Galleria   38
Surrey Docks   39
B23. Wolfe Crescent   39
B24. The Lakes   39
B25. Greenland Passage   40
B26. Finland Quay West   40

C. The East End   41
C1. Lauriston Studios   42
C2. Leyton Fire Station   43
Queen Mary & Westfield College: 44
    C3. Library   44
    C4. Student accommodation   44

D. The West End   45
D1. Embankment Place   46
D2. Sainsbury Wing   47
D3. Sackler Gallery   48
D4. Comyn Ching   49
D5. Stukeley Place   50
D6. Imagination   51
D7. Stevens building   52
D8. Queen Elizabeth II Conference Centre   53
D9. Richmond House   54
The Tate Gallery: 55
    D10. Clore Gallery   55
    D11. Restaurants   55
    D12. Bookshop   55
D13. Crown Reach   57
D14. Vauxhall Cross   58
D15. Channel Four   58
Central interiors   59
Two restaurants:
    D16. Stephen Bull Restaurant   59
    D17. Now and Zen   60
D18. Legends   60
Two disparate shops: 61
    D19. Whistles   61
    D20. Jigsaw   61
Four at Brompton Cross: 62
    D21. Joseph   62
    D22. Joe's Cafe   62
    D23. Issey Miyake   62
    D24. Wilson & Gough   62

E. Heading north 63
West of Regents Park: Marylebone,
Paddington, and beyond 63
E1. Regent's Park villas 64
E2. The Mound Stand 65
Three in Lisson Grove: 66
   E3. Michael Hopkins' office 66
   E4. Lisson/Bell Street Galleries 66
   E5. Lisson Grove offices and flats 67
E6. Saatchi Gallery 68
Four by Jeremy & Fenella Dixon: 69
   E7 Ashmill Street housing 69
   E8. Clifton Nursery 70
   E9. Lanark Road housing 70
   E10. St Mark's Road housing 70
E11. Lancaster Road offices 71
Around Kings Cross 72
E12. ITN 74
E13. British Library 75
E14. Grimaldi Park House 76
Around Battle and
Winchester Bridges: 77
   E15. Bridge Wharf 77
   E16. Regent's Wharf 77
   E17. Porters South 78
   E18. Porters North 78
East and north of Regents Park:
Camden and Kentish Towns 72
E19. TV-AM 79
E20. Sainsbury supermarket and housing 80
E21. Agar Studios 81
E22. Two houses by David Wild 82
Four more in Camden: 83
   E23. Jazz Café 83
   E24. Bruges Place 83
   E25. Crowndale Centre 84
   E26. One Off Studio 84
Around Hampstead Heath and beyond 85
Five private houses: 87
   E27. Burton house 87
   E28. van Heyningen/Haward house 88
   E29. Blackburn house 88
   E30. Weinreb house 89
   E31. Nightingale house 89
E32. Coutts Crescent 90
E33. Highgate Group Practice 90
E34. Bisterne Avenue apartments 91
E35. Walthamstow Coroner's Court 92
E36. Epping Town Hall 93

F. Going west 94
F1. Thames Wharf Studios 96
F2. St Mary's Church, Barnes 97
F3. The Ark 98
F4. Metropolis Studios 99
Stockley Park: 100
   F5. (A1.2, 1.2, 2.1, 2.3) 101
   F6. (A3.1, 1.3, 2.2, 3.2, B1,5,7) 101
   F7. The Arena 101
   F8. (B3) Norman Foster 102
   F9. (B8) Ian Ritchie 102
   F10. (B2/B4) Troughton McAslan 102
   F11. (W3) Eric Parry 103
F12. Bedfont Lakes 104
F13. Richmond Riverside 105
F14. Sterling Hilton Hotel 106
F15. Homebase 107
F16. Fowler/Jestico house 108
F17. Knight house 108
F18. John Lewis department store 109

G. South of the Thames 110
G1. Imperial War Museum 112
G2. Lambeth Community Care Centre 113
G3. Foster offices 114
G4. Bricklayer's Arms 115
G5. Doctor's surgery 116
Two housing projects in Brixton: 117
   G6. Vining Street housing 117
   G7. Strathleven & Mauleverer
      Road housing 117
G8. Carshalton Theatre 118

H. Transport architecture 119
H1. Waterloo International Terminal 119
H2. Stansted Airport 120
H3. East Croydon Station 121
H4. Redhill Station 121
H5. Tottenham Hale Station 122
H6. Bridge Control Room 122
H7. Docklands Light Railway stations 122

Index of architects 123
Index of buildings 125
Photographic credits 127

Preface

From recession to boom – and back again

The prompt for this book was to provide a guide to the wealth of architecture recently completed in London – a remarkable period between the recession of 1981 and the more profound one of ten years later. Perhaps it should have been entitled *From Recession to Recession*, but this would have lent negative overtones to a period which underwent an extraordinary boom in construction activity and produced more than a few excellent buildings.

Unlike previous (pre-Thatcherite) decades, the majority of notable activity during the 1980s was commercial and private, rather than residential and public. There was no equivalent to the French centralist tradition serving the vanity of politicians with *grands projets*, nor the regional independence and competition-producing phenomena such as the rash of new museums in Germany. Burgeoning entrepreneurial and corporate activity was the most significant source of architectural commissions.

Places to work featured prominently, in part because the service sector continued to expand (as a percentage of the working population, for example, the number of professionals is now almost the same as the number of manual workers) and the office became the workplace, enjoyed by unprecedented numbers of people .

As a building type, offices suffer an association with speculative activity during the earlier boom period of the 1960s. The paradigm in many people's minds is provided by *The Apartment* – the movie in which Jack Lemmon inhabits a bureaucratic world of desks in serried ranks, cleared at the end of the day and their telephones placed top-centre . But the offices of the 1980s were different. They were affected by information technology, new concepts of what an office building is, of what an organisation's needs are, and, especially in the case of the City, by the deregulation of financial services. All this led to a flowering of commercial post-modernism and to obsolescence in the older buildings.

A related feature of the period was an increase in the importance of interior design. The fitting out of office buildings for disparate tenants (lending each tenancy a particular sense of identity and place), together with a retailing boom and a fashion for 'signature' design gestures, helped to promote interior design as a major area of activity, forcing architects to reluctantly lend it new acknowledgement. And, on another note, towards the end of the period the recession brought to the fore government-funded architecture serving medicine, transport and civil engineering projects.

Aesthetically, however, the 1980s were significant as a period when post-modernism and its classical variants became not only a fashion, but also a political factor of profound concern within the architectural profession. Although the term is now somewhat moribund within the profession, the spirit of post-modernism became firmly established. The work of CZWG, for example, admirably illustrated a response to the pressures transforming architecture into just another commodity; and the work of John Outram illustrated a post-modern tendency to lend architecture theme and narrative. More politically, Prince Charles and his apologists lobbied energetically and sometimes surreptitiously to promote reactionary architectural values.

The politics of aesthetic posturing became polarised between a post-modernism best represented by the neo-conservative or outright anti-modernist architecture of SOM, Terry Farrell and Quinlan Terry, and the establishment-approved hi-tech of architects such as Richard Rogers, Norman Foster and Michael Hopkins, as well as Farrell's ex-partner Nicholas Grimshaw. It was noticeable that deconstruction – influential abroad – failed to make an impact within British practice (possibly because of rooted anti-intellectual sentiments), although what has been termed Ted Cullinan's 'romantic pragmatism' can be argued to bear an aesthetic affinity with, say, Gunter Behnisch's work in Germany. On the other hand, there was a move during the 1980s toward unadorned, unfinished and undecorated constructions which literally and metaphorically reasserted architecture's substantiality and its designer's assertion that detail is important: aspects of a new direction, neither post-modern, classical nor modernist hi-tech.

Jim Stirling

Outside easy categorisation or stylistic posturing lies the work of the late Jim Stirling, who could be counted upon to offer architecture another kind of substance (real mime, as it were, rather than pantomime) and whose practice with Michael Wilford completed the Clore Gallery in 1986.

The period produced other notable arts buildings in London besides the Clore: the Sainsbury Wing at the National, the Sackler Gallery at the Royal Academy, and the Saatchi Gallery in St John's Wood, the latter by the excellent architect Max Gordon, who also died comparatively recently. In contrast to work in contemporary France and Germany, however, all these examples relied upon private funding.

An important background factor to practice during the 1980s was a deregulation of the architectural profession, producing a widespread move to corporate formats, a more commercial attitude and, for some firms, quotation on the unlisted stock market. Corduroy was put aside in favour of dark double breasted business suits, symptomatic of another nail into the coffin of disinterested professionalism. But without this adaptation much of the profession would have been exposed to another significant aspect of the 1980s boom: the wholesale arrival of rapacious US practices such as SOM, responsible for much of Canary Wharf, half of Broadgate, and Ludgate Place, besides other large office work in London.

All these factors informed the architecture of London during the last ten years.

More prosaically, it was during this same period that London's M25 orbital road was completed. Although metropolitan life in London is an increasingly complex and regional phenomenon, the principal convenience of the M25 to ourselves, as authors, is that it offers (with three exceptions) a useful outer boundary for the content of the guide (although, interestingly, most of the featured work is still within London's historic core).

The content of the guide is based upon many years of guiding architects and architectural enthusiasts around cities and buildings, from Helsinki to Tokyo. These programmes were organised under the umbrella of Architectural Tours, an enterprise set up in 1980 by Victoria Thornton with the overt aim of enjoying the real experience of architecture (and with the secret agenda of getting architects out of their armchairs, away from their magazines and out to the real thing).

AT has always had a natural focus on *contemporary* architecture as the current aspect of a historic dialogue each generation is called upon to engage in. Architecture viewed in this way is more than buildings: it is an acknowledgement of the way we communally make and remake our cities and is inextricably entangled with many factors. However, in the final analysis, something purely architectural stands apart. Other considerations are important, but – to the architectural enthusiast, at least – they should not blind one to the essential architectural experience.

It is in this spirit that we offer this guide to contemporary London. It is dedicated to all architectural enthusiasts – both the producers and the users – but particularly to those who have participated with us in *Architectural Tours* over the last twelve years or more: the architects, interior designers, engineers, doctors, nurses, solicitors, housewives, teachers, archaeologists, software specialists, chemists, bankers and others; the students and the retired; the British and the foreign. Special mention has to go to those who know who have returned again and again to engage in an architectural dialogue and to support our enterprise.

Special mention goes, too, to the guides who have assisted us: people like Bob Allies, Martin Mead, Martin Spring, Andrew Cowser, Nick Rowling, Robert Adam, Richard Weston, and many others.

We also thank all the practices who have offered material for the guide: – you have been very supportive.

We must emphasise, however, that the guide is not a gazeteer and if some work is not mentioned or not discussed fully enough, it is simply because it did not fit our criteria, our editorial policy or (more likely) the space our publishers have allowed. Editing was sometimes difficult and, in the final cull, over-riding importance has been given to the interests of the readership rather than the architectural profession.

Perhaps interior architecture has suffered most. We would like to have given it the extra space it justifies but, apart from editorial and publishing issues, many examples are private or tend to disappear even before they can be published. Hopefully, the works we cite will still be there when you go to look for them.

Thanks, too, to those who have commented upon the selections: you have probably found much to disagree with, but we fly an eclectic flag which acknowledges many varieties of excellence. They are all valid.

Finally, thanks to our publishers, to Edward Pittar and Mark Owen – both excellent and entirely reliable assistants – and to Jo Darke for the inestimable value of her encouragement and editorial advice.

Please note: wherever possible, the dates given for the buildings are when completed. Historians usually offer the date when design was initiated, but we prefer the date the architecture engaged itself in the public realm.

Introduction

Steady action – it' s all that matters

An exhibition of architecture in the City of London held in the Spring of 1992 noted that in the period between 1985 and 1993 half of the area's building stock would have been supplemented or replaced. Anyone travelling through this comparatively small sector of the metropolis in the late eighties would have noticed the frantic activity: blocked roads, cranes and helmeted workers everywhere, even at weekends. But half the building stock?

The dynamics of modern cities are not always so dramatic. More often, change is slow, almost surreptitious, like the shifting of sand dunes. There is a steady action: transformations, alterations, variations, deviations – modifications of the urban fabric as outer signals of exchanges and dialogues between inhabitants. Architecture emerges from all this like a crystalline product arising from a schoolroom chemistry experiment: simultaneously ordered and random, somehow magical but, it has to be admitted, not always beautiful (the RIBA's own awards system typically selects 5% of submissions as decent enough to merit a regional award, and one tenth of the latter as worthy of a national award).

Most people find this process opaque. The chemical equation from which an architecture emerges – the array of circumstances and events which prompt a building project, entrains workers, energies, talents and skills into itself and, finally, bears the completed building out of itself – is not always self-evident. In fact, most buildings are the mute bearers of a hidden narrative.

Like any collective activity, the creation of architecture embraces a complex of interacting factors. A building is the product of multifarious influences, individual wills, ways of seeing and ways of knowing. Seen in this way it can be considered as a built memory: an artefact which has materialised out of sometimes problematic, and sometimes opportunistic circumstances.

We don't usually look at architecture in this way – we fail to 'read' buildings as the product of dialogue and negotiation, of difficulty, personal joys and regrets, and sometimes of lamps burning late at night. Architecture is more than simply a matter of configuring space and form. It is something wrested into being by individuals and organisations, by people who have committed themselves to particular acts, consciously or otherwise. The product of this collective effort is a dialogue in which many voices are brought into a form of reconciliation: a particular architecture at a particular time and place in the urban fabric. Thus the architecture we experience embodies its own formative history. Its configuration and character is a manifestation of the concerns and decisions which made it what it is. The difficulty is that this inner narrative communicates itself rather cryptically.

For example, we can directly experience the Lloyd's of London 1986 building – walking around it, through it, seeing it at different times of the day or week, going into it, perhaps exploring the Chairman's suite and the Adam Room on the upper floors. But the building's place in the development of the Rogers practice, its place in the history of the client's commissioning of three custom-designed buildings, its importance within the typology of office buildings, and its controversial acceptance by users, while less tangible, are very real aspects of the architecture's mute substantiality, residing quietly on Lime Street.

Any architecture is like a mime artist: communicating and affecting us by gesture and evocation, by dramatic movement and charm, surprise and seduction. But the performance – not always an artful intervention in the urban fabric – sometimes manifests more pantomime than mime. In fact, many buildings are constructed without either the benefit of artful intent or any consequential value and *significance*.

This idea of value and significance lies at the heart of any guidebook. But, value and significance for whom? For the designers? the client? the users? the builders? the readers? And what do we mean by significance?

Briefly, we have attempted to interpret significance as the architectural manifestation of something more than ordinary communicative and instrumental competence: there has to be an element of virtuosity. There should also be a note of authenticity – an adjudged truthfulness of voice staking claims of validity.

As guidebook authors, we have no hesitation in declaring a particular interest: *this guidebook is for the architectural enthusiast who wants to get beyond an experience of architecture as photographic images in glossy magazines, who wants to experience buildings directly, in themselves. Such experience is a fundamental test and measure of excellence. To experience a building is to engage in a dialogue far more meaningful than can be found in the pages of a magazine.*

But aren't there many varieties of architectural excellence? What one experiences, for example, is sometimes compromised or only partially realised; excellence can be touched upon rather than fulfilled. And there is also a politics of aesthetic judgement which undoubtedly prejudices viewpoints and opinions. Thus there are few buildings generally agreed by consensus to be excellent, and there are a host of the '*almost all right*', or '*small gems*' which are nonetheless valued and significant. All hint at the background history, the aspirations of individuals and their attempts to wrest gold from the dross of circumstance.

True excellence in architecture is not hard to identify, however, even if the denotation arouses politicised controversy and disagreement between camps within the institutional body of architects. Four recent London examples within a single category are the Sackler Gallery by Norman Foster and Partners, the Sainsbury Wing extension to the National Gallery by Venturi Scott-Brown and Partners, the Clore Gallery extension to the Tate Gallery by Jim Stirling and Michael Wilford, and the Saatchi Gallery by the late Max Gordon. Each achieves a standard of excellence, even if the four are quite disparate (feeding the politics of loyalty and self-identification within the architectural community). Each is included in this guide, where our editorial policy is to adopt a deliberately eclectic viewpoint.

Our enjoyment is with architectural excellence as such. We try to avoid taking sides, and see little necessity or virtue in doing so. Our starting point in compiling the guide has been a search for significant patterns within London's architectural dialogue. In the next section we shall outline what these are.

LONDON: significant contemporary dialogues

In any review of the last ten years of architecture in London two things immediately stand out – changes in the Square Mile and in Docklands. Most of the other interesting work is concentrated within an area more or less bounded and served by the Circle Line. The rest of London has peculiarly little of outstanding interest; what there is tends to be on an axis west, toward Heathrow.

The Square Mile

The changes witnessed in the Square Mile during the mid-1980s to early 1990s were significant by anyone's standards. It has been claimed that there was almost a 50% replacement of the building stock and a net gain of some 12% in floor-space. During 1984 some 2.1m. net square feet were completed; by 1991 the annual figure had risen to 7.1m. Most of this capacity was taken up by the financial services sector while the insurance business – a traditional City occupant – decanted to lower-cost locations, vacating some 3.6 m. sq. ft. over the ten years to 1992.

Although the rate of take-up of office space was already declining in 1988, speculative optimism was still driving developers out to the City's boundaries (reaching out to Docklands in the east), across the river to places such as London Bridge City, and to peripheral areas such as Aldgate and Finsbury. Seemingly overnight, the City had become a building site. At weekends, roads were blocked with construction cranes and were frantically being dug-up for new telecoms cabling.

The completion of a new building for Lloyd's of London, in 1986, signalled an architectural change point. At the time, it appeared unlikely such a building would ever again achieve planning permission. The impression was wrong. In a subsequently hectic atmosphere mixing external threat and internal bullish optimism the City's planning policies underwent radical change. The massive SOM-designed arm of Broadgate received planning permission in six weeks and

by 1992 the Rogers practice had another building beginning construction on London Wall.

During the short intervening period a confluence of events effected massive changes in the fabric of the City. Throughout the 1980s, the impact of electronics at the workplace effected a transformation of office architecture. And in 1986 deregulation modified what went on, bringing new players into the financial services market who brought innovative attitudes with them. New kinds of buildings were needed; those of the 1960s and 1970s were patently obsolete – unsuitable organisationally, technically, and culturally. The need was for large floor plates, voluminous servicing capacity and bulk; the emphasis was upon head offices and dealing floors. Expensive finishes became common and the substantiality of granite became a cliché.

1986 was also notable as a low period for vacancies and office space availability in the City. It was around then that plans for Canary Wharf were announced. Countering the threat and catering to demand a huge development was established around Liverpool Street Station (Broadgate). Within the project, a battle of attitudes and styles became evident: between SOM's north American, commercialised post-modernism and Arup Associates' less ostentatious (but more stressed) British functionalism. It was SOM who were to take over as the property developer's champion.

By the end of the 1990s the take-up in space was back where it had been ten years earlier. The recession was becoming deep-rooted, the City was rocked by scandal, and hindsight was adjudging yuppie avarice to have been an unseemly interlude. Nevertheless, the time lag still produced a 1991 completion of some three times as much office space as was produced in 1987 – when, ironically, a three-year peaking of space take-up had begun to decline; by 1991 demand was less than half the still rising supply.

City culture now consolidated itself as the natural heart of things. But architecturally, the fabric of the City had been amended on a scale unseen since the Blitz, Victorian rebuilding, or the Great Fire.

Meanwhile, during a similar period, development temperatures had also soared in Docklands.

Docklands

At the beginning of our review period the East End was burdened by the stigma of derelict docks and competition against the metropolis' historic westward orientation. Its architectural heritage was that of industrial archaeology and it bore a reputation as a characterful place of welfare housing and left-wing local authorities intent on providing the working population with labour-intensive work of a kind formerly associated with the docks, warehouses and a host of related industrial activities, many of them foul and polluting. *St Katharine's Dock* – lying in the shadow of Tower Bridge and the first part of Docklands to be reinvented – clung like a limpet to its boundary with the City, its obsolescent and pretentiously labelled World Trade Centre signalling an early attempt to attract the City eastward.

A key date is 1981, which saw the establishment of The London Docklands Corporation (LDDC), housed within an early Norman Foster dock building for the Fred Olsen Line.

Following the closure of the West India and Millwall Docks in 1980, the LDDC designated the Isle of Dogs a tax-benefit enterprise zone (an area with tax benefits and minimal planning restrictions). This was its flagship (and, more especially, a vehicle for the Government's free-market policies); at its centre, small sheds more appropriate to suburban fringes were constructed. But larger users came east, too: the productive arms of Fleet Street – the *Times*, the *Guardian*, the *Telegraph* and, later, the

Financial Times – keen to take the opportunity of reinventing working practices in large new printing facilities still near the centre of London.

New infrastructure was provided, including the resuscitation of an old rail viaduct for the routing of (low capacity) driverless trains running from the Tower, along past the *terribilità* of Nicholas Hawksmoor's St.George in the East, down into the Isle of Dogs.

Toward the mid-1980s the pace of redevelopment quickened. Surrey Docks on the south side of the river – within minutes of central London – became transformed into a sub-Milton Keynes housing area. As the country swept into an economic boom, building activity swamped the Docklands and swarms of weekend buyers cruised the sites and show flats. A short take-off airport appeared in the middle of the eastern-most docks, the Royals. Ambitious new waves of speculative optimism rippled through Docklands and land values rocketed. Much of this was prompted by Canary Wharf, where developers purchased land at something like a quarter of the reported market value from the LDDC and proposed a gigantic offices scheme for 40,000 workers – a City satellite. Despite fundamental infrastructure issues which prevented other speculators supporting the project, the development went ahead. The ante had been upped. Earlier developments, such as the adjacent Heron Quays, were suddenly ripe for demolition and replacement.

On the south side of the Thames, adjacent to Tower Bridge, a cohesive and intelligently considered part of Docklands took shape at *Butler's Wharf* – an urban block where decrepit warehouses bearing names like Cinnamon

Piers Gough's contemporary best:
Best religious building:
• Isle of Dogs Pumping Station
Most exhilarating way to blow a fortune:
• Lloyd's of London
The British answer to NASA:
   Scaffolding around
   the Albert Memorial
Who had the greater conversion?
• Bracken House
Most underestimated, unbuilt, and posthumous building:
• No.1 Poultry (Stirling)
Best site hut:
• The Ark
Belgo Award for the most edible interiors on the same side of the road:
• Arad Studios, and
• Blackburn House
Gormenghast Prize for gothic fiction:
• Minster Court
Terry Farrell Award for big buildings:
• Embankment Place

Wharf and Spice Quay lend the air an exotic scent. It was here that the new *Design Museum* sported its pristine white image (ironically, a nostalgic homage to the Bauhaus).

The period ended with the imminent demise of the LDDC after a ten year life, references to its flagship as an architectural zoo, and a quiescence marked by property company failures and the bleakness of recession.

The tower of the troubled Canary Wharf project – its phallic, stainless steel bulk glinting impressively in the setting west sun – is a forlorn monument to everything the 1980s stood for. The area it overlooks, however, has some significant buildings: Richard Rogers' Reuters; Nicholas Grimshaw's Financial Times, John Outram's Pumping Station, Jeremy and Fenella Dixon's Compass Point, CZWG's Cascades, Lacey, Jobst and Hyett's Heron Quays, and others.

Other parts of London

The majority of the decade's other architectural activity – outside Docklands and the City – was, on the whole, in the historic heart of London bounded and serviced by the Circle Line. Activity in the rest of the metropolis was sometimes intense but, with few exceptions, almost invariably small scale and incremental.

Much of the construction activity was speculative housing (refurbished, converted, and new) for Mrs Thatcher's home-owning society. Some domestic projects were discretely squeezed into the urban fabric, e.g. those architects created for themselves – houses by David Wild, Richard Burton, van Heyningen and Haward, and others. Unlike the 1960s or 1970s, there was little or no local authority house building and relatively little housing association work, although some practices did get interesting welfare projects built (e.g. MacCormac Jamieson Prichard in Brixton).

In total contrast, three seriously extravagant neo-classical villas designed by Quinlan Terry for the equally seriously rich were constructed in Regent's Park.

John Young's contemporary best
- Sackler Gallery
- Foster at Stockley Park
- Ian Ritchie at Stockley
- The Mound Stand
- Imagination
- No.1 Finsbury Avenue
- Thames Barrier
- Saatchi Gallery
- Design Museum
- Wakaba Restaurant
- Knight House
- The Ark

Nearby, Michael Hopkins provided his clients at the Lords cricket ground with the Mound Stand – a striking example of hi-tech.

Meanwhile, at Charing Cross and Vauxhall Cross, Terry Farrell – arguably the country's most expert post-modernist – designed two large office buildings as riverside palaces – one for commerce and the other, ironically, for the secret service.

Yet another riverside building, by Jim Stirling and Michael Wilford, extended the Tate Gallery. Regrettably, Stirling – perhaps the country's foremost international name and possibly its most outstanding architect – was to die in 1992.

Again in west London and by the Thames, two of London's most well known hi-tech figures – Norman Foster and Richard Rogers continued to run in parallel, and built their own studios as components of riverside developments. These former partners were both honoured by knighthoods, underscoring both the architectural achievements of this approach to making architecture and its political support by the architectural establishment.

Quinlan Terry's opportunity to build by the riverside was a curiously picturesque assembly of sham neo-Georgian offices at Richmond.

Near to Rogers' studios came a late arrival on the office-boom scene which was both fresh and radical: Ralph Erskine's Ark – a Scandinavian poke in the eye at Anglo-American mind-sets (if only it had been in Docklands).

Other significant architecture was less visible: the boom in interior design. But retail interiors for the fashion trade – by designers such as Rashid Din, Stanton Williams, Branson Coates and Eva Jiricna – set new standards. Jiricna, for example, created a series of up-market shop interiors featuring a stunning series of hi-tech staircases.

Another form of hi-tech retail building making its mark in the later 1980s was a Sainsbury supermarket in Camden Town designed by Nicholas Grimshaw, Terry Farrell's former partner. This was near to a significant building by Farrell built some years previously: a garage conversion into studios for TV-AM.

Wider afield

Camden through Kentish Town and out to the area around Hampstead Heath offers more examples of interesting buildings completed in recent years, as does the Paddington / Marylebone area. But then there is a wide area of little interest before one reaches the northern fringe of our area at Epping, where Richard Reid completed a town hall and local authority offices. And much further out again is one of London's most impressive modern buildings: its third airport, at Stansted.

South London similarly has comparatively few examples. The best includes an excellent community hospital by Ted Cullinan, in Lambeth; Arup Associates' conversion work for the Imperial War Museum; and, on the southern fringe of our area, Cullinan's small theatre in Carshalton.

The middle 1980s produced the glint of stainless steel humps traversing the river adjacent to the Royal Docks: the new Thames Barrier – protection, for a while, from the danger of flooding to central London.

The other major piece of infrastructure in London was the M25, a new multi-lane orbital motorway deemed inadequate from the day it was opened. Its route presented an entirely new linear realm of development opportunity for business parks, out-of-town shopping centres, and new 'villages', all exploiting accessibility and the attractions of the green-belt. Ironically, the most positive aspect of this appetite was made evident on England's foul, polluted and toxic backlands, rather than its green and pleasant land: at Stockley Park, a business park adjacent to Heathrow. The development became a monument to free-market development economics and to the civil engineering of land reclamation.

A comparable development on a smaller and less heroic scale took place at Bedfont Lakes, where Ted Cullinan and Michael Hopkins shared responsibility for buildings arranged around a business park version of a traditional London square (actually an infilled gravel pit).

Not far away, adjacent to Heathrow's new Terminal Four, a building was constructed which looks remarkably like an attempt to recreate Foster's Sainsbury building in East Anglia. In fact it is a hotel designed by Michael Manser Associates, perhaps the most original (sic) in London.

Curiously, large areas of the metropolis have little of outstanding architectural merit or interest. In part, this is because any reasonable current definition of the London metropolis now extends to the whole region of the Southeast. But that's the next guidebook . . .

Ron Herron's contemporary best:
• Lloyd's of London
• Mound Stand
• Sackler Gallery
• Temporary building for MOMI (Future Systems)
• Imagination building
• Thames Barrier
• New Waterloo terminal

Terry Farrell's contemporary best:
• No. 1 Finsbury Avenue
• Lloyd's of London
• Sainsbury Wing, National Gallery
• Clore Gallery, Tate
• Whitechapel Gallery
• Embankment Place
• Vauxhall Cross

A. The City of London

The heart of the City is at Bank, and this is a good point to start with any visits. Most of the buildings listed here are within easy walking distance, although Mansell Street and Whitechapel are on the City's eastern boundary and will stretch one's legs a little further. Around Bank you will find Lutyens' No.1 Poultry (Midland Bank), an adjacent Westminster Bank by Edwin Cooper (who did the first Lloyds building), the contentious Mappin and Webb triangle (Belcher), the Royal Exchange (Tite, recently refurbished by Fitzroy Robinson), Hawksmoor's St.Mary Woolnoth, Dance the Elder's Mansion House, and the John Soane/ Herbert Baker Bank of England. In contrast to the City edges (Broadgate, for example), the medieval street pattern still remains around Bank, although it is always under an erosive pressure which incrementally and relentlessly coarsens the urban grain whilst simultaneously decreasing the kinds of difference one experiences.

Suggested Itinerary:
Girozentrale Vienna (A8)
62-64 Cornhill (A9)
85 London Wall (A11)
Broadgate (A2)
Milton Gate (A15)
Alban Gate (A3)
Ludgate Place (A12)

Bracken House (A4)
Queen Street (A7)
Billingsgate (A13)
Minster Court (A10)
Lloyd's of London (A1)
Fenchurch Street (A6)
Whitechapel Gallery (A5)
Insignia House (A14)

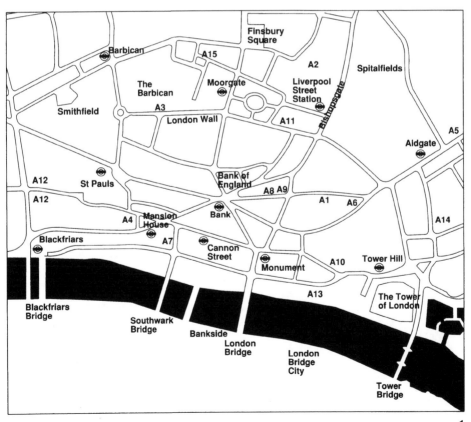

A1. Lloyd's of London, 1986
Leadenhall and Lime Street, EC3
Tube: Bank
Access: private
Richard Rogers Partnership

This exemplary building sits opposite the
Lloyd's 1958 building, designed by Terence
Heysham, and on the site of an earlier Lloyds
building designed by Edwin Cooper in 1927.
The grand Leadenhall entrance portico of the
latter has been retained, accommodating an
uncomfortable junction between the Rogers
building and older, grand manner buildings
fronting Leadenhall. The 1958 building (now
refurbished by DEGW and used for
administrative purposes) doubled the size of the
underwriting room and provided it with a
gallery; the 1986 building enlarged it again, but
this time – being on the smaller, original site –
it was forced to extend the galleries vertically,
within a tall atrium.

Rogers rationalises the building in contextual
terms: a picturesque massing and complex
skyline to blend with the mix of surrounding
buildings; and an urban design concept which
copes with the medieval street pattern of the
City. This seductive narrative disguises a
committed piece of isolated modernism which

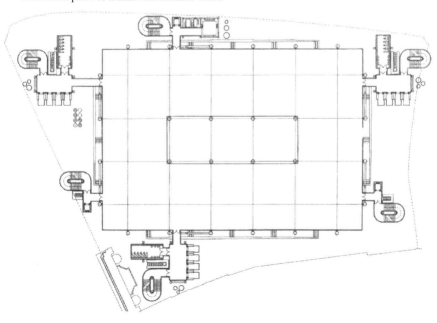

would be equally at home in a green field or on a Docklands site (see Reuters). Its compromised success as a piece of urbanism is epitomised by the lower level concourse beneath the *piano nobile* main floor; this might have extended the urban grain of the adjacent Leadenhall Market (by Horace Jones) but has unfortunately become like some dried-up moat devoid of purpose. Although it contrasts with the 1960s concept of piazza and raised-level pedestrian deck of the Commercial Union building opposite, it is similarly less than successful.

On the other hand, the building's configuration – with its lifts, services and utilities external to workspaces surrounding the internal atrium (the served and servant areas concept) – forms an excellent office building paradigm which is contrary to the dressed-up 'ground-scraper' types which characterised most City redevelopment in the later 1980s (it also cost much more than a conventional office building). The maximum floor plate is approximately 2500 sq.m.

The outside – which has always shocked and delighted in equal measure – retains a startling dynamic character, particularly at night (the lighting scheme is by Imagination). The sophisticated translucent glazing concept, incidentally, owes much to a 1930s domestic antecedent: Pierre Chareau's Maison de Verre in Paris (where the Rogers office was effectively based during the years it worked on the Pompidou Centre, before Lloyd's was commissioned; note also the French-style granite sets to the concourse).

A deep-rooted problem suffered by the building is that it embodies an implicitly egalitarian and non-hierarchical modernist ethic informing a design at odds with Lloyd's culture (one which seeks to be bullishly at an economic leading edge, but to do so in environmental circumstances signalling cultural reassurance and affirmation of its establishment

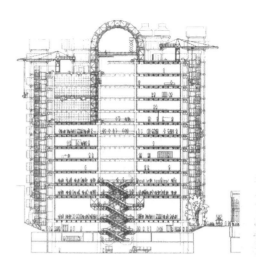

status). Consequently, the original interiors have already suffered controversy and emasculation. In particular, the Chairman's suite – a remarkable place on the upper floors which incorporates the 18th century council room as a mock classical edifice within Rogers' enclosure – is a bizarre conjuncture of robust modernist architecture and whimsical interior design (not by Rogers).

The 5th floor Visitor's Gallery is currently closed but might reopen for recognised groups. A visit allows one to experience all the essentials of the interior and to gain a spectacular view of the atrium – the building's inner focus which the fully-glazed peripheral accommodation overlooks and addresses. One is confronted by an incongruous sight which sums up the building: soberly faced and costumed City-types silently conveyed on escalators across the atrium, ostensibly unaware that beneath their feet the underlying reality of brightly lit and painted inner mechanisms are revealed and displayed for all to see.

A2. Broadgate Complex, 1984-92
Liverpool Street / Bishopsgate, EC2
Tube: Liverpool Street
Access: squares and lobbies only
Arup Associates and
Skidmore Owings and Merrill

Canary Wharf frightened many people in the City, producing radical amendments to complacent planning policies. Broadgate – representing the buoyant market conditions of the mid to later 1980s, the influences of deregulatory forces, and a response to the need for new office buildings providing for information technology – was among the first projects to benefit from such changes.

Broadgate's 3.5m. square feet, lying around and over Liverpool Street and Broad Street Stations (1860–70s), should be read as a large chunk of London redeveloped as a single scheme: a contemporary commercial equivalent of residential comprehensive redevelopments undertaken in the 1960s (e.g. the Barbican). It should also be read as a confrontation between American and British architectural traditions and values, reflecting their respective Beaux Arts and Arts and Crafts roots and sentiments.

Half the scheme comes from the firm of Arup Associates and the other half from the Chicago firm of Skidmore Owings and Merrill (also responsible for much of Canary Wharf). The design vision and drive behind the

development, however, comes from the property speculator Stuart Lipton: the real hero of this development.

The first building on the site was *No. 1 Finsbury Avenue* (1984), situated on Wilson Street, designed by Arup Associates' partner Peter Foggo for an expanding financial services market requiring high-standard, well serviced buildings with large floor plates (on the North American pattern). The 1980s bull market and British Rail's appetite for profits prompted further development. This produced a fine public square in front of No. 1 (in the English tradition of Georgian squares), followed by a circular arena (Broadgate Circle) where most of the few shops and bars of the complex are located. Modelled on the Rockefeller Center in New York, the Circle's central stage is used for lunch-time entertainments in summer and ice-skating in winter.

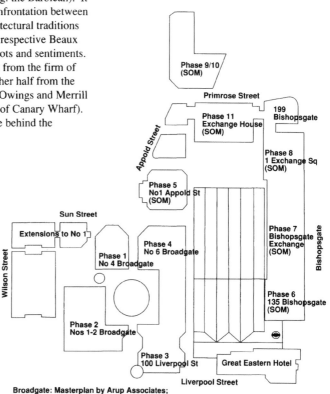

Broadgate: Masterplan by Arup Associates; phases 1 to 4 by Arups; later phases by SOM.

4

The remainder of the development is by the Chicago office of SOM and different attitudes to making architecture are readily apparent. Arup sustains modernist concerns with authenticity, striving to facilitate a meaningful reading of constructional substantiality; SOM, however, were committed to a Beaux Arts theatrical presence by whatever (usually historical) means came to mind. Whereas SOM employ different styles for each building, Arup's have one underlying theme (a simple glazing system) with variations on ways to hang granite. The final building – 100 Liverpool Street – brings this concept to a difficult conclusion and sits in contrast to the undoubted success of No.1 Finsbury Avenue.

Where the development is faced with the challenge of building within the air-rights over the rail-tracks, SOM provide their version of hi-tech: a dramatic exposed steel structure of parabolic arches carrying the floors (Exchange House, Primrose Street). An adapted antecedent for the building is clearly the Federal Reserve Bank of Minnesota by Birkets and Associates. In front of it is the third public gathering area: Exchange Square, complete with sandstone walls reminiscent of H.H. Richardson's Chicago work.

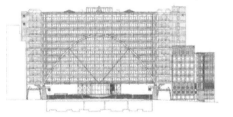

The surprise of the development is the work of British Rail's internal architects (and their engineering consultant, Tony Hunt) who have produced a lively station successfully marrying old and new. The original structure has been artfully and seamlessly extended; the old hotel has been rebuilt so that it becomes impossible to say whether it is old or new; and mock Victorian towers provide ventilation shafts and roof bracing. This work takes inspiration from a variety of precedents: Guimard's metro stations, the work of the Spanish engineer Santiago Calatrava, Lloyd's cast brackets, and contemporary urban design in Spain.

The developers of Broadgate have made an effort to offer significant public art to users, critics and potential tenants. Artists include Richard Serra, George Segal, Jacques Lipchitz, Barry Flanagan, Stephen Cox, Alan Evans, Jime Dine, Xavier Corbero, and Fernando Botero. Mind you, Philip Johnson might still see them as 'turds in the plaza'.

A3. Alban Gate 1991
London Wall EC2
Tube: Moorgate
Access: pedestrian deck and lobbies only
Terry Farrell and Company

Alban Gate is an extravagant post-modern building in peculiar circumstances demanding sophisticated aesthetic and technical solutions. Its site is London Wall, a notorious strip of roadway lined with 1960s commercial slab-blocks where the Barbican confronts the older urban fabric of the City. The block concept was bad enough, but matters were exacerbated by their execution and the absurdities presented by the planner's raised deck separating pedestrians from vehicular traffic.

Farrell had to cope with all this as well as the problem of how to economically redevelop the site of one of these slab-blocks. His answer was to offer two, linked buildings – one spanning London Wall itself. This still left the difficulty of the front door. Where is it? On the deck or where one expects it, or on the street?

Such problems almost overwhelm the undoubted urban design skills of the architects – Alban Gate certainly doesn't feel like a gate to anything or anywhere. But this is not to say that Farrell's design fails. On the contrary, these locked Siamese twins cope almost heroically with their circumstance. The post-modern aesthetic gamesmanship might not be to everyone's taste, but it succeeds in making an expert transmutation of the intrinsic difficulties. Well, almost. At the lower levels, in particular, the handling of the acrobatic structure appears heavy-handed, almost crude; Farrell succeeds marvellously at the upper levels, but not here. But how does one elegantly integrate a po-mo facade into an unavoidable hi-tech expression of the way a large, multi-storey building straddles a roadway? The same problem repeats itself in places such as the atria cladding walls, where the detailing seems inappropriately heavy, as if Farrell is attempting to reinterpret the language of hi-tech. But enjoy this building's virtues – it does have them.

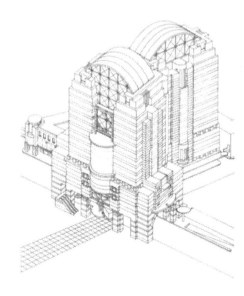

A4. Bracken House, 1991
Friday Street EC4
Tube: St. Paul's
Access: private
Michael Hopkins and Partners

Albert Richardson's appropriately pink Bracken House of 1959 was formerly the home of the Financial Times, before its printing works moved into a building in Docklands designed by Nicholas Grimshaw, and the journalists moved to a nondescript building in Southwark. In their conversion, the Hopkins practice have removed the heart of the building, retained the listed north and south wings, and provided a new doughnut plan office area around a central lift core and atrium (the latter a delightful hi-tech exercise in glass floor blocks and glass lifts riding in plate steel structure – a precursor of what the practice did at Bedfont Lakes for IBM). The inner space has only one row of columns between the core and facade.

The plan acknowledges the inspiration Richardson received from the 17th century Palazzo Carignano in Turin, where two wings are separated by an elliptical entrance block.

On the outside of this rather reticent building Hopkins has provided his Japanese clients with an articulated gunmetal cladding which echoes the geometry of windows on the existing wings. The cladding picks up the deflection of the cantilevered concrete floors and brings their loads down to steel cantilever brackets sitting on stone-faced piers. (These brackets suggest themselves as small-scale

versions of what Grimshaw provided at the Sainsbury supermarket in Camden; one can also detect a family resemblance between Grimshaw's FT building cladding and the way Hopkins stiffens the glass entry screen at Bracken House – but all similarity ends there.)

The public's experience of the conversion is essentially of this sophisticated cladding and it is Hopkins' accommodation of Richardson's earlier work which is part of the delight to this otherwise uncompromising design.

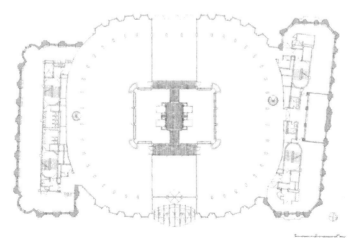

A5. Whitechapel Art Gallery, 1984
Whitechapel High Street, E1
Tube: Whitechapel
Access: Tues-Sun 11am-5pm; Wed 11am-8pm
Colquhoun and Miller

This refurbishment and extension of Harrison
Townsend's Arts and Crafts building of 1901 is
a fine example of Colquhoun and Miller's work
before the partnership broke up. The work is
executed with restraint, although a restricted
budget constrains some of the detailing and
quality of finish. These are simple – a part of
the ubiquitous language of contemporary
galleries, comprising white walls, light wood
floors and preferably no skirting.

The architects have provided refurbished
galleries, a new mezzanine cafe, lecture theatre,
audio visual facilities, book shop, offices, etc.
The work included a new five-storey extension,
described by the architects as 'sympathetic to
the existing fabric, without imitating it'.

All of this is finely achieved in the rather
cool and considered way of all the practice's
work. Much of the design is concerned with the
circulation e.g. the public stair from the main
gallery floor to the upper level gallery. The
latter owes something to most architects'
favourite staircase: the long straight one
designed by Alvar Aalto for the Institute of
Pedagogics in Jyvaskyla.

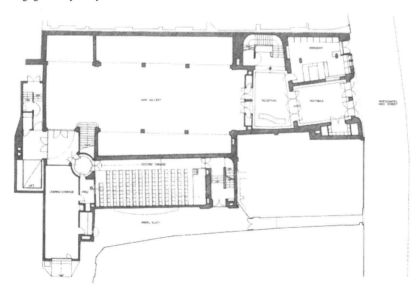

City directions 1: Post-modernism

Two by Terry Farrell:
A6. Fenchurch Street offices, 1987
corner Fenchurch Street and Leadenhall, EC3
Tube: Aldgate
A7. Queen Street offices, 1985
Queen Street, EC4
Tube: Mansion House
Terry Farrell and Company

Two by Rolfe Judd:
A8. Girozentrale Vienna, 1984
68 Cornhill, EC3
A9. Cornhill Offices, 1988
62-64 Cornhill, EC3
Tube: Bank
Rolfe Judd Partnership

Two very English:
A10. Minster Court, 1992
Mincing Lane, EC3
Tube: Tower Hill
GMW Partnership
A11. 85 London Wall, 1989
London Wall
Tube: Liverpool Street
Casson Conder Partnership

Three by SOM:
A12. Fleet Place, 1992
Ludgate Hill, EC4
Tube: Blackfriars
Skidmore Owings & Merrill

The following two sections group together leanings toward two polarised approaches to making architecture: post-modernism (ever an ambiguous term); and hi-tech. If there is a single, outstanding feature of the culture served by post-modernist architecture it is the promotion of its own commodification. This hardly frees hi-tech from such an association, but post-modernism has been more eagerly grasped by speculative developers. It has been termed the architecture of compensatory facades, emphasising an intent to offer reassurance and flattery. It is frequently thematic. The po-mo buildings in the City are all different, but all betray an agenda concerned with image-making, place-making and packaging equivalent.

A6. Fenchurch Street offices

Access: Ground floor during banking hours
This corner building at Leadenhall and Fenchurch is characteristic of Farrell's work. The building effectively identifies an eastern entry point to the City and serves to underscore the architect's expertise in this kind of situation. The parallel is with his work at Comyn Ching in Covent Garden – where a play on corners also constitutes a large part of the architecture. At Fenchurch Street, Farrell plays an elaborate, layered and hierarchical game which links and interpenetrates the elements of the corner, and then tops them with a circular boardroom.

A7. Queen Street offices

Access: private
Another interesting building by Farrell is in Queen Street. The *parti* provides a minor facade in the side street, Skinner's Lane, and a major facade to Queen Street. The latter is conceived as twin pavilions to the scale of adjacent buildings; these are linked by the portico and (another) rooftop level boardroom. The cladding bears Otto Wagner references.

A8. Girozentrale Vienna

Access: private

These two office buildings in Cornhill represent a revival of the grand manner common in the inter-war period. As smaller infill reinforcing the street and block in the manner of Lutyens nearby bank building (140–4 Leadenhall, 1929) they stand in contrast to Lloyd's further east, and the enormity of Broadgate further north.

This Viennese bank at 68 Cornhill is overtly thematic, bearing the influence of Otto Wagner's architecture in Vienna to underscore its occupant's origins.

A8

A9. Cornhill offices

Access: lobby only

Judd's other building at 62–64 Cornhill is a well-executed attempt to replace a 1911 listed building on the same site. The practice has expertly employed pre-cast concrete technology, allowing large-scale panels with Portland stone facings to be strapped to the ubiquitous steel frame. Horizontal and vertical joints have been carefully integrated into the modelling of the facade, offering one of the best examples in London of this approach.

A10. Minster Court

Access: courtyard and lobbies only

GMW's *Minster Court* – a new home for insurance sector head offices (insurers decanted from the City on a massive scale during the 1980s) – was potentially a marvellous piece of Disneyland: a large, deep office building pretending to be a cathedral and ironically paying unconscious homage to mammon.

There is real expertise in this popular building's massing and facade treatment, giving it prominence on the skyline and presence in the street. But the architecture suffers from a failure of nerve: it's not cathedral-like enough. The gigantic steel and glass canopy over the entrance forecourt – whose structure is not as hi-tech and advanced as cathedrals were – recalls a provincial bus station rather than something sublime; and the diminished scale of the entry lobby seems both unfortunate and inappropriate.

The building is worth comparing with others by GMW in the City, offering an idea of how much has changed in the last twenty years.

A9

A10

A11. 85 London Wall

Access: private

As an office building, Minster Court represents
current trends toward block-filling
'groundscrapers' for large organisations. In
contrast, Casson Conder's comparatively small
office building at 85 London Wall, near
Broadgate, is orientated more toward the
professional than the banking or insurance
sectors. The building admirably exemplifies an
anachronistic strain of mainstream architecture
about which there is something peculiarly
English and collegiate – modernism's
interpretation of a quintessential kind of
Englishness. Similar work has come from the
offices of William Whitfield (e.g. the DHS
building in Whitehall) and Powell and Moya
(e.g. the Queen Elizabeth II Conference Centre,
opposite Westminster Abbey).

The building has been deliberately
designed with a deceptively complex-looking
modulated facade of stone-clad pre-cast panels.
The roof line has been set back in order to
reduce the perceived height.

A11

A12. Fleet Place

Access: lobbies only

Fleet Place is a complex of three buildings
designed for Rosehaugh Stanhope. It comprises
50,000 sq.m of floor space and occupies a long,
winding site that was formerly a rail corridor
leading to a bridge straddling Ludgate hill and
blocking the view from the west to St Paul's. In
a major civil engineering feat becoming a
familiar association with Stanhope, the bridge
was removed and the lines pushed underground.

A12

Most of the designs temper SOM's pot-
boiler approach to post-modernism, but still
adopt the 'styling is an historical dustbin'
approach to aesthetics. No. 1 Fleet Place is an
exercise in exposed structural steel framing; No.
10 is an exercise in black granite and stainless
steel, its verticality and pinnacled parapet line
giving it the air of something late medieval or
Perpendicular in style; No. 100 adopts a more
familiar po-mo language with late Victorian
overtones.

The other dimension to SOM's work is
the place-making that goes on in linking
Ludgate Hill to Holborn Viaduct.

A12

City directions 2: Hi-tech

A13. Billingsgate Securities Market, 1988
Lower Thames Street, EC3
Tube: Tower Hill
Richard Rogers Partnership

A14. Insigna House, 1991
83-85 Mansell Street, E1
Tube: Aldgate
**Elana Keats & Associates/
John Winter & Associates**

A15. Milton Gate, 1991
1 Moor Lane, EC2
Tube: Barbican
Denys Lasdun, Peter Softley and Partners

Hi-tech has become a dominant theme in the politics of British architecture. The term refers to designers who like to adopt a leading-edge posture, seeking out the new and technically novel. There is always the pretence – sometimes disingenuous – that limits are being extended, that the conversation is being pushed.

The approach manifests technological optimism and concerns to create a technologically derived aesthetic founded upon an instrumental rationale. At a time when most architects are becoming increasingly weaker members of the design team, it also promises to empower them against the onslaughts of those who would reduce architecture to commodification and cosmetic packaging. It offers architects a particularly strong grasp of one kind of authenticity. Unsurprisingly, there are not many examples in the City. Here are three variations.

A13. Billingsgate Securities Market
Access: private
Billingsgate Fish Market was moved to Docklands in 1982. This left a late Victorian building by Horace Jones (also responsible for *Leadenhall Market*, behind Lloyd's, and the architect of *Tower Bridge*) looking for a purpose in life. Revitalisation became possible in the mid-1980s when it was purchased by Citicorp with the idea of converting it into dealing rooms and providing a boat link across the Thames to their other offices in London Bridge City.

The Rogers practice carefully repaired the existing structure, went underground and coped with the permafrost of the Thames mud, where frozen fish had been stored since the 1870s, and provided two new mezzanine floors – one within the vaulting, the other hanging from the original structure of the ground floor. This ground floor (a 3000sq.m space) is particularly good, but the underground cafeteria level would have been rather dreary.

Then, in 1987, the market changed and Citicorp had no need of the facility. Since the building had been purpose-designed into the largest dealing facilities in London at substantial expense (£20m for 11,200sq. m), it hardly lent itself to other than dealing-room purposes, and so remains empty.

You can peek through the windows to get a glimpse of what Rogers achieved.

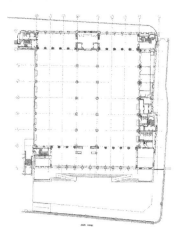

A14. Insignia House

Access: private (lobby only)

This 3000 sq.m. building, designed by John Winter in collaboration with Elana Keats, is a clean and simple exercise in creating a small office building suitable for either a single tenancy or multiple lets, and in the making of effective facades and impressive entrance areas.

The plan is a simple rectangle squeezed between two party walls, with all service areas arranged to one side. At the top is a glazed penthouse office space.

An abandoned requirement for street widening prompted a negotiation with the planners to allow an atrium to project 3m in front of the building line. This serves as a 25m. high entrance lobby, thermal barrier, and acoustic baffle to the busy road. To one side is a glazed wall-climber lift.

The building is a model of simple rationality and constructional control.

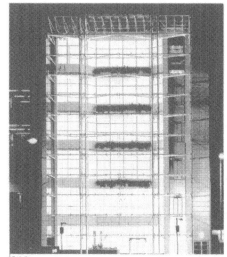

A14

A15. Milton Gate

Access: private (lobby only)

This bizarre 20,000sq.m office building near to the Barbican is by the practice of one of the UK's foremost post-war architects, Denys Lasdun (designer of the National Theatre).

The architect describes his design as a building in search of elemental qualities and a formal intensity – a building employing a castellar metaphor of turrets, towers, a central drum, a steeply pitched upper roof, and a veil of glass. The plan is a simple doughnut floor plate with a central atrium; in its midst arises a circular service core.

The building is both literally and metaphorically green, being entirely clad in a deep, double-skin of glass (compare with Foster's ITN). On the other hand, some people find it all rather alienating and poorly constructed. If only the greenness had included a warmer consideration of people, or had plants on the building, as were used by Arups at Broadgate, around the corner.

Along the street the Barbican Centre by Chamberlin Powell & Bon can be found which clearly shows change of attitude to materials between the 1970s and 1980s.

A15

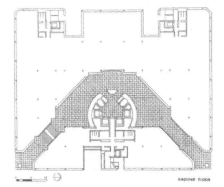

A15

B. Docklands

Throughout the 1980s Docklands was the largest area of urban regeneration in Europe, raising many questions about valid urban forms, valid social policies and valid political process – issues which appear to be recurring around Europe in similar situations. Although latterly ensnarled in a recession which ground development efforts to a halt, there is nevertheless much to experience and review. It is a unique phenomenon and needs to be experienced if only for that reason.

The LDDC – administratively responsible for the redevelopment programme – has undoubtedly been successful in many ways – significant capital and development enterprise have been attracted to the area. But its excessively optimistic faith in the capacity of the market to provide a civilised urban place is highly questionable. Apart from its offer of attractive financial and planning benefits, ostensibly free from bureaucracy and local politics, the LDDC's notion of its enabling role relied upon free-market development politics, limited infrastructural interventions, framework planning and bizarre urban design concepts such as prescribed landmark buildings. Above all, market criteria were dominant, producing results which have been widely castigated as an architectural zoo.

But what is a valid programme of process and order when regenerating a city? What makes for viability, relevance, coherence, justice and reassurance? And organicity?

The best areas to visit are the Isle of Dogs, Wapping, and Butler's Wharf. At the time of writing, the Royals, in the east, have little of architectural interest (including the short take-off airport) although there is a pumping station by the Richard Rogers practice which needs to be contrasted with John Outram's rather different building in the Isle of Dogs serving a very similar purpose.

The easiest way to get around is by car or private coach but Wapping, Limehouse and the Isle of Dogs can be accessed from the Docklands Light Railway. However, be warned: it is less reliable, frequent and convenient than one is led to believe; nevertheless it is the easiest way to get from Bank or the Tower of London Underground stations. Once there, be prepared to walk if you want to see everything we have noted. The Rotherhithe Tunnel provides an alternative link to Butler's Wharf on the south side of the river. Among its architectural attractions, Butler's enjoys a Conran restaurant and the Design Museum offers somewhere for refreshments.

The best of old architecture in the area are Hawksmoor's churches and the remaining industrial archaeology of the warehouses and docks which bear witness to 200 years of economic and social history. Unfortunately the latter is fragmentary: now fractured, fissured and overlaid with nostalgia. Many docks have been infilled, their defensive and impressive brick walls demolished and the robust warehouses neglected, burnt or gentrified. The clues are there; it's just that you'll have to put the pieces of the jigsaw together yourself. In the process, consider why wholesale redevelopment in the 20th century – whether it be visionary or predatory – never seems to fulfil its optimistic promise or substitute for incremental and organic change.

Docklands breaks down into three principal areas of interest:

*• **The Isle of Dogs***
The flagship of the LDDC's promotional enterprise and the place where some of the best contemporary architecture is located.

*• **Wapping and Limehouse***
Two of the more characterful areas, largely (and ironically) because they retain a viable urban community living in an established framework of streets.

*• **Butler's Wharf and Surrey Docks***
Essentially a single city block which is possibly the most coherent part of the entire docklands area. London Bridge City is nearby. In Surrey Docks there are a few residential developments to see.

B. Docklands – Isle of Dogs

Isle of Dogs and Royals
Heron Quay (B1)
Canary Wharf (B2)
Cascades (B3)
Ferry Street (B4)
Compass Point (B5)
Stewart Street Pumping Station (B6)
Royal Victoria Dock Pumping Station (B7)
Financial Times (B8)
Reuters (B9)
Isle of Dogs Neighbourhood Centre (B10)
Thames Flood Barrier (B11)

Wapping and Limehouse
Roy Square (B12)
Shadwell Basin (B13)
Tobacco Dock (B14)
La Lumiere (B15)
Butler's Wharf and Surrey Docks
Horselydown (B16)
Design Museum (B17)
David Mellor building (B18)
Saffron Wharf (B19)
The Circle (B20)
China Wharf (B21)
Hays Galleria (B22)
Wolfe Crescent (B23)
Lakeside (B24)
Greenland Passage (B25)
Finland Quay West (B26)

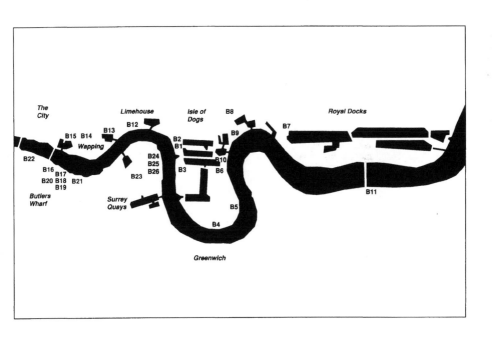

The Isle of Dogs (and the Royals)

A new, north/south access road and the Docklands Light Railway both run down the central axis of the Isle; round the heartland of docks runs an older perimeter road. One can walk to all of the projects mentioned from Docklands Light Railway stations, although a car makes life easier. Pick up the Light Railway at Bank or Tower Hill underground stations. The southern half of the Isle is mostly of residential – constituting a history of British housing from the 1930s through to the 1990s.

Suggested Itinerary:
Heron Quay (B1)
Canary Wharf (B2)
Cascades (B3)
Ferry Street (B4)
Compass Point (B5)

Stewart Street Pumping Station (B6)
Royal Victoria Dock Pumping Station (B7)
Financial Times (B8)
Reuters (B9)
Neighbourhood Centre (B10)

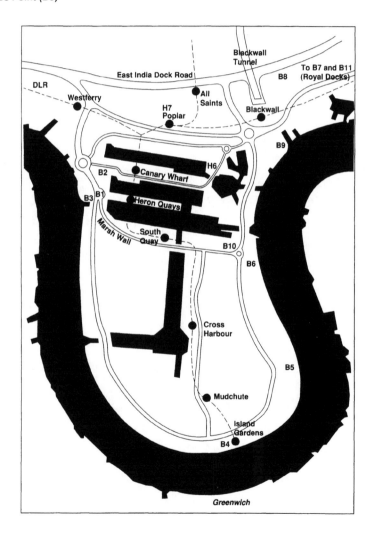

B1. Heron Quays development, 1984-8
Heron Quays, Marsh Wall, E14
DLR: Heron Quays
Access: private (lobbies only)
Nicholas Lacey Jobst and Hyett

Heron Quays – a complex of small office and studio units – suffers from blight because of the possibility that it will be demolished and replaced by something akin to one of the adjacent Canary Wharf buildings. This will put an end to a history of less than ten years and is evidence of a series of ever larger waves of speculative optimism which overran Docklands in the later 1980s.

The design employs a vaguely Scandinavian aesthetic of large, metal sloping roofs and cladding, together with an open-ended feel which suggests robustness and adaptability. A principal virtue of the buildings is the way they welcome the visitor: bringing one over the water's edge, opening up a view to the dock, allowing one to walk along a waterside access deck. The experience could be characterised as maritime, but without it falling into a banal pastiche of something ship-like (a recurring thematic cliché with which some architects seem obsessed).

Canary Wharf – standing opposite – fails to embrace any of these possibilities.

The buildings sit on a strip of quayside which is a third of a mile long and only 50m wide. In Lacey's words the scheme 'was an ambitious attempt (against the odds) to stitch together at least one coherent piece of urban fabric . . . a place of a sympathetic scale making the most of its superb watery surroundings'. The slenderness of the site was 'a pretext for launching the scheme out into the docks themselves, half in and half out, lending the building an amphibious nature, dramatizing the relationship with the water'.

Only the first two phases were ever completed before the development was overshadowed by Canary Wharf. It was originally to be a fully mixed-use scheme with apartments and shops as well as offices.

Further south of Heron Quays along West Ferry Road is an interesting water sports centre designed by Kit Allsopp.

B2. Canary Wharf, Phase One, 1992
Cabot Square, West Ferry Road, E14
DLR: Canary Wharf
Access: public areas only
Skidmore Owings and Merrill
Cesar Pelli & Associates
Kohn Pederson Fox Associates
Pei Cobb Freed & Partners
Troughton McAslan
Hanna Olins (landscaping)

Canary Wharf was once intended to provide
1.23million sq. m of office space. It is unlikely
ever to be considered the most significant
development of the 1980s, but its 45-storey
tower might well become the most popular.

Intended as a satellite of the City, Canary is
a place of large, US-style office buildings with
heavily serviced, deep floor spaces. The
complex is almost entirely an American import
– with smaller European elements (only one has
been realised) as window dressing to SOM's
beaux arts master plan. The main Canary
buildings, for example, are stone-clad
'groundscrapers' designed by the transatlantic
practices of SOM, Kohn Pederson Fox, and Pei
Cobb Freed (the same who gave Paris the
Louvre); the stainless steel-clad tower and the
shopping building faced in exotic sandstone are
by Cesar Pelli, well known for the 'blue whale',
another large building in a low-rise context, in
LA. The landscaping is by Hanna Olins and
construction management is by Lehrer
McGovern – both US firms. Even the majority
of construction materials and components are
from abroad. Apart from the design of a
smaller building on the north side of the tower
by Troughton McAslan, not much is British
except the sweated labour.

The initial development goal was to reach a
viable mass as soon as possible: buildings,
roads, services, shops, transport access,
marketing programme, and so on, including the
trees, bushes and turf of the landscaping.
Instant city. It was a stupendous task.

The outstanding building (literally and
metaphorically) is the Tower. It is impressive
from almost anywhere in London, but not from
close to, and especially not from within a lobby
haunted by security guards who, until the
viewing gallery was briefly opened to the
public, were in the habit of enforcing a
Tarkovsky-like no-go zone between the street

doors and the lift core which takes one (or some) to some inner sanctuary.

But is this your idea of a valid urban place? Or an office? Or somewhere to eat and shop? Such a complex cannot organically change and adapt; being dedicated to restricted purposes and functions, it is always in danger of becoming a dinosaur. Socially, difference is precluded by managerial policy and control, squeezed out, and relegated beyond the Canary boundaries. Don't attempt to misbehave.

Nevertheless, it is remarkable – go there. But you'll be forgiven for a sigh of relief on return to the comparatively humane realities of central London.

The architects for the buildings are as follows:

A. 1 and 7 West Ferry Circus (north side)
Skidmore Owings & Merrill

B. 1 Cabot Square
Pei Cobb Freed & Partners

C. North Colonnade
Troughton McAslan

D. 10 and 25 Cabot Square
Skidmore Owings & Merrill

E. 20 and 30 Cabot Square
Kohn Pederson Fox

F. No. 1 Canada Place, the station and Cabot Place (the shopping building)
Cesar Pelli & Associates

Two buildings designed by Aldo Rossi (with Perkins & Willis) and another by Koetter Kim Associates are planned but currently on hold.

To the east of the Canary tower building is a bridge with a control tower by Alsop & Stormer, 1991 (H6).

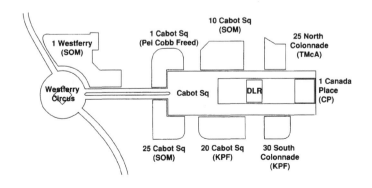

Three housing developments

B3. Cascades, 1988
2-4 West Ferry Road, E14
DLR: Heron Quays
CZWG

B4. Ferry Street, 1982
Ferry Street, Millwall, E14
DLR: Island Gardens
Levitt Bernstein Associates Ltd.

B5. Compass Point, 1986
Sextant Avenue, off Manchester Road, E14
DLR: Island Gardens
Jeremy Dixon/BDP

B3. Cascades
Access: private
This is the 20 storey CZWG building which once made it to the front cover of British Telecoms A-K listings. In the designer's words, 'Cascades is anti-pop, or is it? What, after all, could be more despicable than high-rise living – architects would hate it, the public would hate it. We just had to do it. Then it sold brilliantly'. One doubts if any speculator would back such a rationale, but it makes a good story.

The architecture features a mix of nautical and Victorian warehouse themes. The imagery alludes to marine design: portholes; steel balconies intended to be like those on a lighthouse; ship-like funnels for flues, and the like. The cladding brickwork is intended to appear as if a new building was pushing its way up through a fictional existing warehouse – a metaphor for the redevelopment of Docklands.

A great virtue of the design is the way it provides scale to such a large and prominent building.

Next door is the Anchorage residential development by Michael Squire Associates

B4. Ferry Street
Access: public
This is one of the better small housing developments in Docklands – a mix of single storey units for the elderly and three storey units for families. The 46 dwellings are formally arranged in a V formation on an axis to Greenwich and the Cutty Sark, yet the overall impression is anything but formal.
Refreshingly, there is an avoidance of the effete neo-vernacular which characterises much of the housing in docklands.

The design (for a housing association) is informed by an egalitarian policy which sets the terraces at an angle to the Thames so that everyone gets a view. Appropriately, the overall aesthetic is rather Scandinavian, employing corrugated aluminium roofing and timber siding. It is all very pleasant, very humane and very well designed.

Unfortunately, the scheme has two major faults: the walkway on the riverside goes nowhere; and the scheme is possibly too modest for such a significant site.

B3

B4

B5. Compass Point

Access: public and river walk streets

Compass Point and Ferry Street are two of the better designed housing developments in Docklands, but they are quite different. Ferry Street is a housing association project and rather Scandinavian in feel, owing much to public housing programmes of the 1970s; Compass Point is a design and build project of private houses cultivating 18th-century themes. Both schemes are formally arranged on axes.

Pedestrians enter Compass Point from the street through a tall slit in a half-circus of town houses replete with a white, rendered facade and neo-Regency balconies. Front and back are clearly differentiated.

Directly in front, across the river, are the huge grain silos of a sugar factory; and on either side of this axial view Dixon has designed similar half-round features to the end of terrace houses. The reference is to the modernist celebration of North American industrial architecture during the 1920s and 1930s. But this is the only modernist note in a scheme whose other references are to the stucco architecture of John Nash and the Regency Tuscan villas and terraces of west London.

These contextual notes are typical of the Dixon's work. Its peculiar Englishness, however, makes it difficult for some foreign visitors to appreciate.

It is worth relating this scheme to the Dixon's preceding housing work in West London, some of whose features are incorporated into Compass: the river terrace relates to St Mark's Road; the central avenue of villas to Lanark Road; and the minor court to the north is similar to Ashmill Street.

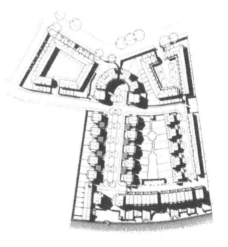

Between Ferry Street Housing and Compass Point is the Edwardian pedestrian tunnel under the Thames to Greenwich on the south side.

Two pumping stations

B6. Stewart Street Pumping Station, 1988
Stewart Street, E14
DLR: South Quay
John Outram Associates

B7. Royal Victoria Dock Pumping Station,
1987–8
Tidal Basin Road, E16
DLR: Under construction
Richard Rogers Partnership

These two buildings could hardly be more different, yet their purposes are similar: both pump rainwater run-off into the Thames. Their only other commonality is a penchant for bright colours.

So far as aesthetic preferences are concerned, one is tempted to suggest that you take your pick. But it is not that simple.

The Rogers building is all steelwork, pipework, industrial railings, ducts and other paraphernalia of the hi-tech approach to making buildings, wrapping two concentric drums rising 12m above ground and twice as far below. The designers argue for the boldly detailed and brightly coloured surfaces, steelwork and services on the outside as overcoming 'the remote and unfriendly characteristics commonly found in municipal/unpeopled buildings of this type'.

John Outram adopts a different approach. As an architect, he defies categorisation: thoroughly modernist in his attitude to construction (although hardly a radical, like Rogers), and a committed post-modernist in his approach to architectural meanings. His building is given an almost arcane allegorical narrative: snow in the mountains (pediment), water from the cave (circular exhaust vent), a stream through the forest (the columns), a river over the plain (coloured blocks). In substance, the building accords with modernist concerns to offer a functional, readable and honest construction: what you see is what you get. The large fan exhausts methane gas build-up; the column shafts house storage and utilities; the circular side vents ringed with 'Roman' tiling allow ventilation air in, and so on.

The bright colouring is reminiscent of a Chinese pagoda, or perhaps some late 19th-century Beaux Arts drawing of a Greek temple. In the same tradition, it appears to bear celebratory homage to the Abbé Laugier's evocation of the natural origins of classical architecture – something at once rude and intelligent, fundamental and erudite, robust and dignified.

Whereas the Rogers building celebrates technology and its instrumental nature, Outram's focuses on an entirely different set of cultural values which appear richer, and perhaps with more potential to stir our emotions. But appearances tell only a part of the story.

When one looks at the fundamental parti employed by each design, the position is reversed. The Rogers design unabashedly grasps the nettle of the engineering functions and produces forms deriving from a truly creative response to providing the screen chambers, discharge chamber, pump hall, control room and so on. Outram, on the other hand, is less interested in such matters and is clearly happy to offer a cultural edifice whose narrative takes priority over the engineering functions. Both work equally well. Together, they say much about architecture, but choosing between them is surely pointless – better to simply enjoy the juxtaposition.

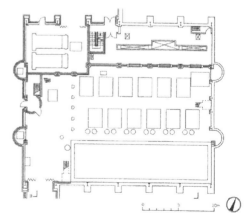

B6. Stewart Street Pumping Station

Access: private (Thames Water)

Outram's temple to pumping water incongruously sits midst a 1960s housing estate on the corner of Stewart Street and – believe it or not – Folly Walk.

Outram has also designed a row of five terraced warehouse units in Kensal Road, W10 (1980).

B7. Royal Victoria Dock Pumping Station

Access: private (Thames Water)

Rogers' pumping station sits on a roundabout at the western edge of the Royals and is meant to also serve as a landmark building and gateway to the Royal Docks.

B8. Financial Times Printing Works, 1988
240 East India Docks Road, E14
DLR: Poplar
Access: private, but tours can be arranged for groups
Nicholas Grimshaw & Partners Ltd.

There is often something acrobatic about Grimshaw's hi-tech architecture (see Waterloo Station, the Sainsbury supermarket in Camden, and the Homebase near Heathrow) – a striving to employ the constructional facts of life as the basis of architectural form and to make a case for technology. The results are invariably good, but court the accusation of a wilfulness which, ironically, is close in character to a similar quality in the work of his former partner, Terry Farrell.

The best time to see the *Financial Times* building is at night, when the glass frontage becomes a public window on the processing of huge rolls of pink paper. In fact, this is the principal part of the building that arouses the observer's interest.

This frontage extends a shed-cladding conversation initiated by Grimshaw in the 1970's, when 80% of project effort went into inventing a cladding package – something at once novel, innovative and full of image-potential.

In this instance the inventiveness has produced large external steel fins which –

typical of Grimshaw's buildings – work overtime both as structural and image-making features. As well as supporting an eaves beam, they are the principal components of the wall of glass stretching between the blank east and west service wings. The outriggers which reduce the glass spans fulfil their function with clarity and vigour. It is an impressive gesture, repeated on the rear, entry facade.

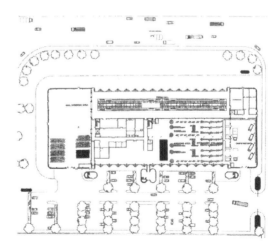

B9. Reuters Technical Services Centre, 1989
Blackwall Yard, Gaselee Street, E14
DLR: Poplar
Access: private; access to street; public walkway
accessible only via prior trespass
Richard Rogers Partnership

Perhaps the Reuter's building is a poor man's
Lloyd's. The building similarly places core
features such as lifts and stairs on the perimeter,
is of a similar scale to the City building and,
like Lloyd's, it provides its *piano nobile* on the
first floor. However, Reuter's is without the
benefit of the generous Lloyd's budget or
Rogers' expertise on the fit-out. It is also
without a central atrium, is largely given over to
telecommunications equipment, and is
apparently populated almost entirely by security
guards rather than the crowds of a marketplace.

The electronics are evidenced by blank
cladding and a large green steel superstructure
on the roof which accommodates the air
conditioning plant. The security consciousness
is evident in an acutely medieval, defensive
quality reinforced by the security fence; the lack
of a front door (just a security hut and a massive
cantilevered gate which silently glides shut);
and the strategic riverside position straddling a
former dock entrance. It is rumoured that the
building has multiple electrical back-up systems
in the form of duplicate generators and links to
the distribution grids on both sides of the river.

In front of Reuters – on the riverside
approach side – is a stretch of public walkway.
But to get to it one has to trespass upon a
temporary car park area and risk being chased
by the security guards before the sanctuary of
the river's edge can be reached. It's all rather
bizarre.

Reuter's has an outpost in the form of a
fully glazed restaurant block set to one side.
Raised on a stack-bond block base, this elegant
two-storey building offers its users wide-open
views up and down the river. They then dive
back inside the citadel.

Given this state of affairs, the public
walkway will probably continue going from
nowhere to nowhere – an inaccessible political
sop to public sentiments.

B10. Isle of Dogs Neighbourhood Centre, 1992
Jack Dash House, Marsh Wall, E14
DLR: South Quays
Access: public, Monday to Friday
Chassay Architects

Not many town halls get built these days. This one – ranking as the country's first purpose-built neighbourhood civic centre – accommodates local town hall services and various community facilities for the London Borough of Tower Hamlets, who thus re-establish its presence in territory formerly taken over by the LDDC. It's not the equivalent of Aalto's Saynatsalo town hall, but is one of the few meritorious buildings in Docklands. Its funding, incidentally, was a planning gain from the Canary Wharf development.

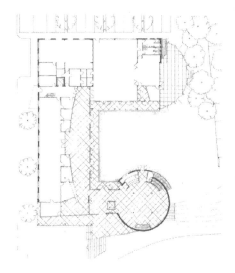

The building's *parti* has three components: a circular council chamber block – separated from the rest of the complex so as to symbolise the democratic freedom of the councillors from the bureaucracy (Tower Hamlets has split its council into neighbourhood committees); an oblong, five storey office block (with obligatory curvy roof); and a square-plan community hall block of two storeys. Both of the latter are white rendered blocks raised up on piloti.

These three units are arranged in a C plan around a courtyard, with the brick-faced rotunda of the council chamber acting as landmark on the corner of the site. Unfortunately, this landscaped court has been closed off by a council fearful of its vandalising constituents. But the ground floor of the rotunda is a public exhibition space and most of the ground floor of the oblong block is freely accessible to the public. The latter has a 'circulation hall' shaped by a long curving, blue wall which faces onto the court through a glazed wall.

As a project, the centre was marred by contractural difficulties generated by a design and build contractor going into liquidation. Fortunately, Chassays Architects had by then successfully achieved most of their objectives.

B11. Thames Flood Barrier 1982
Royal Docks, E16
DLR: under construction
Access: none, but visible from Royal Docks
Rendel, Palmer and Tritton (Engs.)

Flooding is not that unusual in London's history; as recently as 1928, for example 28 people were drowned in Westminster basements. The city has sunk 15 ft since Roman times; this fact, together with a possible combination of severe weather and high tides makes the possibility of devastation to 45 square miles of central London an ever greater threat. The result would a disaster of enormous proportions.

The answer has been proposals for a series of flood gates straddling the river. This was first suggested in the 1850s and reiterated in 1904 when a proposal for dock gates at Gravesend was put forward. Similar proposals – complete with a topside road – were made in 1934.

The present barrier is a big machine spanning 520 m. Four main shipping lane gates of 3000 tons lie on the river bed awaiting the danger signals to be hoisted into position. Each is 61m wide and rises 20m above the river bed.

Six secondary gates flank them. Between each gate are concrete piers housing electro-hydraulic equipment sheltered beneath elegantly shaped stainless steel forms. They have certainly made a dramatic alteration to the riverscape.

Wapping and Limehouse

Apart from the Isle of Dogs, the other architecturally interesting area north of the river in Docklands is Limehouse and Wapping.

The principal contemporary attraction of Limehouse – the area just west of the Isle – is a scheme by Ian Ritchie: Roy Square. (Its other main attraction is Hawksmoor's St Anne's.)

Wapping is the area nearest to the City. It is bounded by the river to the south, by the Highway to the north, Shadwell Basin to the east, and St Katharine's Dock to the west. It is an area of character and, like Limehouse, it also enjoys a Hawksmoor church – St George in the East, opposite Farrell's Tobacco Dock Stanton Williams have a scheme to make radical internal amendments to the building).

The key route through the area is Wapping High Street, which formerly gave access to the warehousing along the river. An alternative is to follow a canal-side walk that starts at Tobacco Dock and terminates near to St Katharine's; it runs through a not unpleasant neo-vernacular housing area.

Suggested itinerary:
La Lumiere (B15)
Tobacco Dock (B14)
Shadwell Basin (B13)
Roy Square (B12)

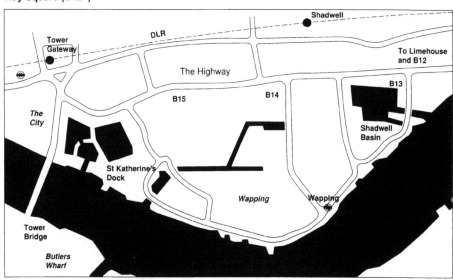

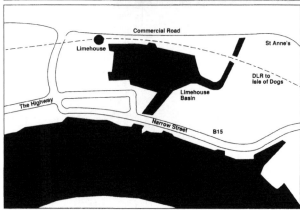

B12. Roy Square, 1988
Narrow Street, Limehouse, E14
DLR: Limehouse
Access: private
Ian Ritchie Architects

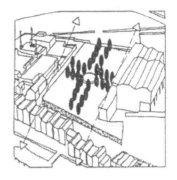

So many architects visit this building that a security hut now gates access to its inner garden – but you can usually get close enough to see without trespassing or upsetting the residents. The attraction is one of the few residential developments in Docklands that is neither a historical pastiche nor neo-vernacular. Although it is without the overt historical references offered by Jeremy Dixon in his housing projects (see, for example, Compass Point), Roy Square nevertheless employs similar concerns with tradition, the rationality and the civic values informing Georgian architecture.

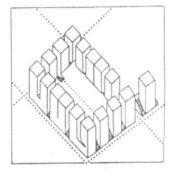

The development is an urbane block of town houses and apartments. Because aspect is generally so dreary, the apartments are ranged around an excellently landscaped inner court set upon a raised deck; parking is below. This terracing is rhythmically fractured to articulate the units and allow as much daylight to penetrate as possible.

The making of the scheme is the landscaped court, without which it could be overbearingly dense and rather cold – qualities underscored by the use of light coloured, very regular brickwork. The geometry of the facades are carefully regularised – just as a Georgian house would have been. But there is also a cool quality to this artfulness – one which suggests an emphatic rejection of warmth and irregularity. Nonetheless, the architects have realised an elegant and considered architecture rich in civic consciousness.

The Grapes pub is situated across the road for weary feet!

B13. Shadwell Basin 1988
Glamis Road, Wapping, E1
DLR: Shadwell
Access: dockside walkway open to public
MacCormac Jamieson Prichard

This is a design and build scheme of 169 houses and apartments by the practice of the 1991–3 RIBA president. The scheme wraps itself around the basin, seeking to provide it with a comparatively dense urbane edge to what has been considered as a watery London square.

However, the original concept had to be diluted because it would have adversely affected winds onto the basin – intended for water-based recreational sports. This requirement also demanded that the terracing be fractured in order to let winds penetrate down onto the water giving the architects an opportunity to articulate the individual dwellings.

The design owes something to the aesthetic of load-bearing brickwork, strips of vertically aligned loading door and dock-edge arcades that one once found at St Katharine's. However, this is no pastiche, but rather a worthy appropriation and transmutation of an anachronistic aesthetic.

(The strident red, by the way is a product of a design and build project management concept which denied the architects control over detailed specifications.)

Nearby are two other interesting developments: New Crane – a warehouse conversion into apartments by Conran Roche; and Pelican Wharf by Shepheard Epstein Hunter. The former betrays modernist loyalties informing their conversion work. Pelican, on the other hand, adopts the format of converted warehouse (complete with light well), but is a new building.

The Prospect of Whitby pub is also between these two buildings for those in need of a rest.

B14. Tobacco Dock 1990
Pennington Street, E1
DLR: Shadwell
Access: normal shop hours
Terry Farrell and Company

Daniel Alexander and John Rennie's Tobacco
Dock is an excellent example of late Georgian
design. Apparently Karl Freidrich Schinkel was
impressed, too. The lower level brick vaulting
and the upper level timber trusses are minimal,
exact and elegant – the hi-tech of its day.

The bays of the present shopping centre
have been expertly restored, refurbished and
converted. In contrast to the original, however,
Farrell's steel and cast iron insertions are
heavily redundant – yet they work.

On the upper level, the steel angles and
large sheets of glass provide both robustness
and transparency; at the lower level, the cast
iron assemblies – incorporating doors and fire
shutters – have a more opaque (and
Dickensian?) feel. The latter make a not
inappropriate infill to the original, richly
coloured vaulting which springs from elegantly
shaped stone piers. In both instances there is an
assertiveness about Farrell's designs which
establish a successful dialogue between old and
new. The manner in which the existing heavy
brick security walling surrounding the
warehouse is penetrated has also been well
handled.

It is when Farrell employs romantic neo-
Piranesian features to the central steps between
upper and lower levels that the project slips
toward a regrettable theming (heavy, riverbank
stonework, complete with huge steel rings,
ostensibly for mooring vessels). The developer
independently pushes this deplorable theming to
a kitsch apogee in a steel 'galleon' sited in the
former London Dock. Come back Disney, all is
forgiven.

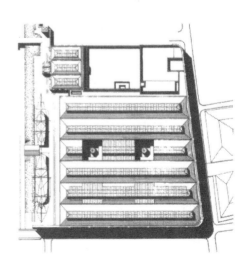

*Opposite Tobacco sits the robust but
forlorn shell of Nicholas Hawksmoor's excellent
St. George in the East, for which Stanton
Williams have a scheme.*

B15. La Lumiere, 1991
2 Pennington Street, E1
DLR: Shadwell
Access: private
Rick Mather Architects

This is an office building developed by an architect turned speculator: the late Michael Baumgarten.

Mather's design knits itself into the urban fabric, offering strong frontages both to the Highway and to Pennington Street (where the main entrance is). The building is two blocks around a central landscaped courtyard which rises through five storeys. This allows two major sub-tenancies on each of the main floors (further sub-division is possible).

Each facade is developed on a theme. The Highway frontage rakes the cladding wall from end to end, exposing structural columns. This copes with a misalignment between adjacent properties. Layers of set-back balconies are topped by a huge projecting canopy penetrated by large oculi. This is an early Parisian, modernist device; here, it gives the block a strong identity, but appears somewhat over-scaled. A tall, thin glass feature signals where the central escape stair rises up the building (there is a similar feature on the Pennington Street facade); this also serves to indicate the entrance.

The significant feature of the Pennington Street frontage is a five by five set of triangular, projecting windows over the glazed entrance canopy. This face of the building is set at 45° to allow for rights of light; one half of the triangular window is obscure glass in order to prevent overlooking. The uncharacteristically slim Roman bricks of this facade are specially made in Germany.

Front and rear blocks are linked by a lobby linking both and providing access to the central lifts. Within the office spaces, floor to ceiling heights are low and, thankfully, without a suspended ceiling. Air conditioning is within the raised floor zone, but it is also designed so as to allow users to open windows. In fact, the building is highly energy efficient.

Westwards along The Highway is the
Thomas More Complex by Sheppard Robson.

Butler's Wharf and Surrey Docks

Butler's Wharf is a relatively small urban block adjacent to Tower Bridge. One can walk from here all the way along the Thames, past Hays Galleria to the South Bank cultural centre and beyond; it's worth doing.

Butler's Wharf itself is a large, late Victorian warehouse built in 1874. It sits on the river side of Shad Thames, a narrow street once filled with goods traffic winding its way beneath overhead bridges linking riverside and inboard warehousing. The building has now been converted into 98 luxury apartments and the street has been excellently restored (all by Conran Roche). It has to be admitted, however, that the resulting pristine and fragmentary quality serves to underscore how much of docklands has disappeared and how the remainder has been themed. The ground floor of the buildings is set aside for speciality shops and restaurants, fronting Shad Thames and the river.

At one end of Shad Thames is the picturesque Anchor Brewhouse (converted into residential units by Pollard Thomas Edwards), and Julyan Wickham's Horselydown; at the other is the modernist Design Museum. Beyond that is CZWG's China Wharf and New Concordia Wharf. These sit around an inlet which once provided access for barges and now has new buildings such as Hopkins's Mellor Building and Conran Roche's Saffron Wharf; at its head is Michael Squire's white residential tower, Vogan Mills.

Suggested Itinerary:
Butler's Wharf
Horselydown (B16)
Design Museum (B17)
David Mellor Building (18)
Saffron Wharf (B19)
The Circle (B20)

China Wharf (B21)
Hays Galleria (B22)

Surrey Docks
Wolfe Crescent (B23)
The Lakes (B24)
Greenland Passage (B25)
Finland Quay West (B26)

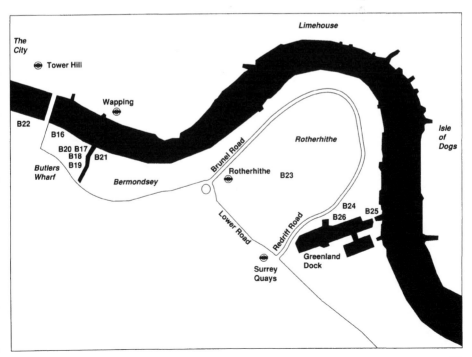

B16. Horselydown development, 1991
Horselydown, Shad Thames, Bermondsey, SE1
Tube: London Bridge
Access: public
Wickham Associates

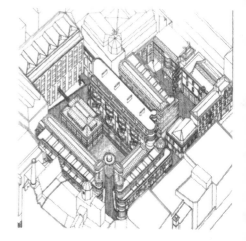

This is one of the better pieces of architecture in Docklands, by an architect formerly best known for bars and restaurants. Its aesthetic character is personal to the point of verging on the idiosyncratic, having vaguely Dutch and de Stijl overtones. This style is quite unlike others currently in vogue, although it enjoys some parallels: a concern with constructional authenticity, with simple and ordinary finishes, and with hi-tech features (such as the galvanised stairs), etc.

Parts of this large building complex (170 apartments, offices and shops, and parking for 300 cars) are compositional delights – for example, the southwest corner, adjacent to the pub – but the whole complex occasionally has a gargantuan quality in danger of escaping the architectural language. Some find the large inner court, for example, somewhat overbearing. Perhaps it should have had large trees in it, even if this would have complicated the car parking structure underneath. As a bare, Italian style piazza it doesn't really work (compare with the very English square created by Arups at Broadgate).

The side street near Tower Bridge and the old Courage Brewery is more successful, echoing the smaller scale of the old warehouses in much of the Butler's Wharf area. On the other hand, the Shad Thames facade copes well with the bulk of Butler's Wharf itself. The ground floor of the shop units, which are glazed front and back, allows a visual link between street and inner court.

If you like Wickham's work, also see his small block of flats in Bisterne Avenue, Northeast London; the Le Champenois, and Corney and Barrow restaurants in the City (1985); and Kensington Place restaurant (1987).

34

B17. Design Museum, 1989
Shad Thames, Bermondsey, SE1
Tube: London Bridge
Access: Tues-Sun 11.30am-6.30pm; Thurs to
9.30pm
Conran Roche

This was formerly a postwar concrete frame warehouse looking like most other warehouses in Docklands. By the time Conran Roche had finished, the dreary building had been transformed into a clean, white homage to the International style of the inter-war years – looking as if Gropius had designed it in 1932.

All this is rather ironic for a forward-looking institution celebrating the role of design in modern culture and industry.

The purpose of the building is to explain the function, appearance and marketing of mass produced consumer goods. To do this, the building provides exhibition space, lecture hall, shop, library, and cafes. The man behind it all is Terence Conran.

The building looks splendid and pristine, fronting a river terrace. If it has a fault, it is that the interior organisation does not immediately reveal the exhibition spaces, so that the interior does not explain itself or even invite one through. There seems to be a curious disparity and discomfort between the building and its content, which ranges from the display of a watch to that of a car, or graphics, industrial machinery, and so on. Their relationship seems incidental, even contrary, leaving Stanton

Williams – who were responsible for the collection exhibition – to sort matters out.

Outside the Museum, on the riverside, is a striking sculpture by Paolozzi. Behind the Design Museum is a similar large warehouse conversion by Allies and Morrison (the Clove Building). They have also transformed an old building's image by cut-outs, set-backs, a new arcade, balconies, a white render finish, and so on.

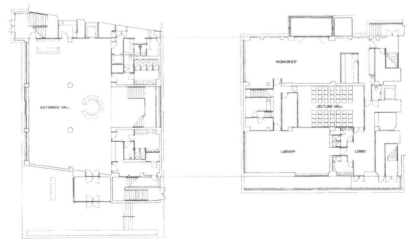

Two small office buildings

B18. David Mellor building, 1991
Shad Thames, Bermondsey, SE1
Tube: London Bridge
Michael Hopkins

B19. Saffron Wharf, 1990
Shad Thames, Bermondsey, SE1
Tube: London Bridge
Conran Roche

*In some ways these two small buildings on Shad
Thames are very similar; in others, they
contrast greatly. They are about the same size
(17,000 sq.ft for the David Mellor building;
24,000 for Saffron) and fit not dissimilar
waterside locations. Both buildings employ
large areas of floor to ceiling glass on their
facades. But while it is the David Mellor
building which appears more constructionally
interesting and is the richer visually, it is the
Conran Roche building which establishes the
strongest presence midst the area's old
warehouses of similar scale, particularly when
seen from the river side (walk beyond the
Design Museum and look south into the inlet
basin).*

B18

*Hopkins' design offers a reticent
architecture characterised by the grey colours
of its exposed concrete and lead cladding. No
doubt it will age and mellow rather well. In
contrast, Conran Roche's design is clad in
glossy, white stove-enamelled panels and stands
forth as a pristine comment upon its more worn
and weary older neighbours.*

B19

B18. David Mellor building 1991
Access: normal shop hours
The Hopkins plan provides a clean geometry to
the floor plate. Toilets, services and escape
stair are accommodated in the irregular north
side; the south side is more regularly and
formally arranged with a separate main stair and
lift tower.

B19. Saffron Wharf
Access: private
The plan of Saffron Wharf is comparatively
conventional, although, like the Mellor
Building, it makes a point of glazing both street
and waterside frontages.

Two by CZWG

B20. The Circle, 1989
Queen Elizabeth Street, SE1
Tube: London Bridge
Campbell Zogolovich Wilkinson & Gough

B21. China Wharf, 1988
Mill Street, SE1
Tube: London Bridge
Campbell Zogolovich Wilkinson & Gough

*CZWG's work is vigorously image orientated
and characterised by a search for cheap and
cheerful features of the kind relished by
speculative developers and sales agents. Their
reputation is for opportunistic and jokey
architecture. They protest at this and ask to be
taken seriously, but the labelling (and its
insinuations) sticks. In fact, they are very
expert. And very serious about what they do.*

B20. The Circle
Access: private
In the case of *The Circle* – a large scheme of
302 apartments – there are three of these
features which strike the visitor: a dominating
circular arrival court emblazoned with
startlingly blue tiles reaching up to gables, with
a vaguely cartoonish profile, as if a giant owl
ominously threatened – a profile apparently
intended to be like giant vases; a vigorous
patterning of the facades by balconies which are
ostensibly propped by rudely cut tree trunks;
and a large sculpture of a dray horse lending a
note of historical authenticity and reassurance
(the site used to stable such animals).

Inside – where architectural image making
provides little contribution to added value, and
interior designers take over – the flats are,
unfortunately, rather ordinary, failing to fulfil
the lively promise of the facades.

B21. China Wharf
Access: private
China Wharf (its impressive frontage is best
seen from the river side, just beyond the Design
Museum) is a smaller CZWG offering of 17
apartments, pleasing to many people besides
British Telecom, who put the building on the
cover of their L–Z listings. As expected, the
joke is there: the lowest of the central row of
balconies is the severed stern of a boat, intended
to appear as if disappearing beneath, through
heavy supporting piers.

B21

B20

B21

B22. Hays Galleria, 1986
London Bridge City, Tooley Street, SE1
Tube: London Bridge
Access: Mon-Sun 6.00am-11.30pm
Michael Twigg Brown & Partners

Hays Galleria forms a part of London Bridge
City – a mid-1980s office development
stretching from London Bridge toward Tower
Bridge. Like other developments (the most
notable of which is Canary Wharf) it extends
the City boundaries by creating satellites – in
this case, across the river.

The principal building (its gateway as
urban designers euphemistically say) is by the
John Bonnington practice and sits on the corner
where the riverside development meets London
Bridge. It is a large, square-plan office block
with a cut-out corner vaguely reminiscent of the
Ford Foundation building in New York (except
that, here, there is no enclosed atrium). It
doesn't work because its scale is daunting rather
than human and welcoming, and its mirror glass
facade is alienating.

Hays Galleria is more successful. It sits
in the centre of the development, adjacent to the
entirely different offices of Citicorp, who
intended running a boat ferry for their staff
between here and Billingsgate opposite.

The Hays building was originally a
Victorian warehouse wrapping a barge inlet
basin where goods could be loaded and
unloaded (similar to that still existing at New
Concordia Wharf, just east of Butler's Wharf).
This has been infilled to provide a new public
place and covered with a sheltering glass roof
which opens onto the river. The warehouse
itself is now an office building. What has been
realised is a good place to enjoy on a river
perambulation between the South Bank and
Butler's Wharf, although this is fairly dead
outside office hours.

*It has fine views across the river to
Billingsgate and the City and is a good place
for refreshments.*

Surrey Docks

B23. Wolfe Crescent, 1989
Canada Street, off Quebec Way, SE 16
Tube: Rotherhithe
CZWG

B24. The Lakes, 1990
Norway Dock, Redriff Road, SE16
Tube: Rotherhithe
Shepheard Epstein and Hunter

B25. Greenland Passage, 1989
South Sea Street, off Redriff Road, SE16
Tube: Rotherhithe
Kjaer Richter

B26. Finland Quay West, 1989
Onega Gate, off Redriff Road, SE16
Tube: Rotherhithe
Richard Reid

Most of the Surrey dockside warehousing and much of the docks themselves are gone. The largest remaining stretch of water is Greenland Dock – a vast and rather barren stretch of water. Thus we have unfortunate demolition and infill matched with a failure to soften and humanise the residual industrial element. Despite this, there is architecture worth visiting.

The Greenland Dock Control Building by Conran Roche is worth seeing; it is comparable with the Alsop & Stormer bridge control building in the Isle of Dogs.

B23. Wolfe Crescent

Access: private
CZWG's scheme of 53 dwellings adopts the confident form of a four-storey crescent of 26 townhouses, facing four octagonal apartment blocks (like individual villas) arrayed along a diminutive canal. Squeezed onto a corner of the site behind the crescent (nothing is wasted) is a fifth apartment block. The four apartment blocks provide 'affordable' accommodation for local authority tenants (a planning gain).

The crescent includes double garage entrances as semi-circular arches formed from pre-cast concrete units in the shape of frilly curtains. And there are chimneys, too – although they appear unable to accommodate any kind of flue.

B24. The Lakes

Access: private
In contrast to Wolfe Crescent, Shepheard Epstein and Hunter's (artificial) lake side development is less cheerful and jokey, but possibly more satisfying. If the water feature is a throw-away gimmick, then it is a well considered and executed one. It gives the development an introverted character offering a human scale in contrast to the adjacent open spaces designed for ships – a design sensitivity which could have benefited other developments around the dock and which is quite rare in the whole of Docklands (Heron Quays is an exceptional example).

Semi-detached villas around the lake make up most of what has been completed (the full scheme is for 177 dwellings). They are reassuringly well designed and constructed, offering considered plans, workable arrangements, proper thresholds and suchlike – what one expects.

B23

B24

B25. Greenland Passage

Access: private

Kjaer Richter's scheme is for 152 dwellings arranged in four blocks around a communal, landscaped court; the car parking is underneath.

Like Richard Reid's scheme, Greenland suffers from a concept which has difficulty coping with the exposed location. In these terms, the Lakes has both the advantage of being away from the water's edge and being a more considered design without large windswept areas overlooked by large blocks. As Reid's scheme, the development suffers from the developer once again failing to understand the importance of good detailing (and placing too much emphasis upon an odd, historical rationale).

Apart from this, the Kjaer Richter scheme attempts something more urbane than most of the housing in Surrey Quays.

B26. Finland Quay West

Access: private

The Finland Quays scheme is a row of seven linked pavilions (what architects quaintly term a necklace) of 67 dwellings forming an edge to the quay. Its architect, Richard Reid, is an excellent designer, but his design takes on a strong challenge in addressing the barren openness of Greenland Dock.

The architecture is very good. However, Reid has lifted the dwellings above the dockside walkway, exacerbating exposure to the austerity of the dock. One longs for some intermediate detailing which might promote the quayside as a place to linger – to inhabit, no less. This, together with the meanness of detailing brought about by a design and build contract, brings a bereft and forlorn quality to an otherwise good design. Landscaping might help.

C. The East End

Unlike the equivalent area in Paris, London's East End has surprisingly little of contemporary architecture to see. The little there is to see is also spread out.

Colquhoun & Miller (now John Miller &

Partners) have two small examples of housing infill here, one of them near to the best piece of architecture in the area – by a young practice, Patel and Taylor (a scheme worth comparing with Penoyre and Prasad's doctor's surgery in south London).

Suggested Itinerary:
Lauriston Studios (C1)
Leyton Fire Station (C2)
Queen Mary & Westfield College Library (C3)
Queen Mary & Westfield College student accommodation (C4)

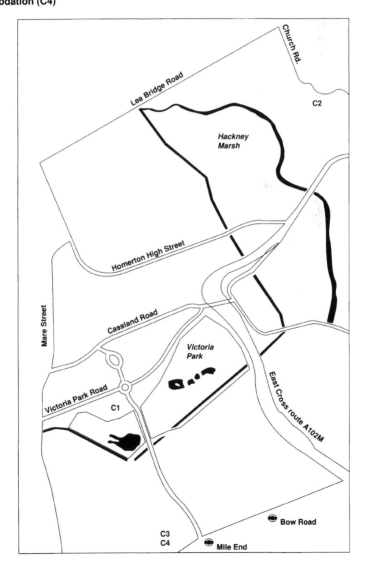

C1. Lauriston Studios 1990
Connor Street, off Lauriston Road, E9
Tube: Bethnal Green
Access: private (by arrangement)
Pankaj Patel and Andrew Taylor

This conversion of former stabling set between rows of 19th-century terrace housing is one of the better examples in London of what skill, inventiveness and perseverance can achieve with a minimal budget and against the opposition of planners and neighbours. The result – against all odds – is a superb piece of gritty architecture (as well as a bench mark of what determination and stamina can achieve).

There is little to see outside: merely a simple transformation of the former stable gates into a glazed frontage. The surprise is inside – in a long, irregular space where a central mezzanine structure and perimeter toplighting are the key features of the interior.

The architectural configuration is largely dependent upon the necessity to carry all the central mezzanine's loads on a structure independent of the crumbly perimeter walls (formerly without foundation and, as party walls, not allowing side windows).

The mezzanine platform itself is a real bit of hi-tech wood-butcher's art (if that is not a contradiction in terms). It is a plywood stressed-skin design with an elegant section, executed boldly and simply, without a refinement of finish.

The building is used for shared work-spaces and includes wall space given over to exhibitions of local artist's work. The street building has been converted into a shared meeting space.

Just north of the Studio, at Church Crescent, is some semi-detached housing by Colquhoun and Miller – interesting, but forbidding.

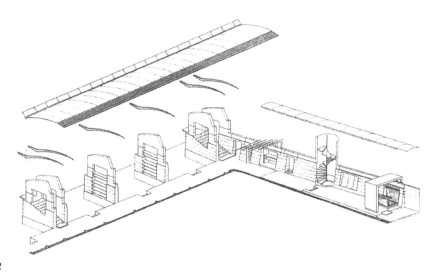

C2. Leyton Fire Station, 1991
Church Road, E10
Tube: Leyton
Access: by arrangement
Rock Townsend

Rock Townsend's London work varies from a large, speculative office building in Islington (Angel Square), pretending to be four or five disparate pieces of architecture (Frank Gehry meets SOM), to buildings like this: a local fire station more in the tradition of their community work such as the Crowndale Centre in Camden Town.

Firemen are a down-to-earth breed. It then comes as no small compliment that the unit at Leyton are more than satisfied with their building. True, it replaces something apparently less than adequate; but Rock Townsend's station is a model of good organisation, draining the brief and the project's tight budget of architectural potential.

Together with its tall practice tower – topped by a pyramidal roof – the building stands out above the roofs of adjacent two storey terraces as a rare example of civic architecture which, 150 years ago, might have been a church.

There are two principal components to the building's *parti*: accommodation for the engines; and a separate accommodation block

for the firemen. The latter – complete with slide-down pole from the dormitory and mess areas – stacks two walls of multi-storey accommodation around a spacious atrium overlooking the appliance bays. This is the main circulation space. It drops into a basement area where there is a gymnasium and waiting area. The former is greatly appreciated, but the latter is sadly underused – apparently because the local authority are anxious about their liabilities if visiting school children and the like have an accident. So much for dialogue with the community. This is all the more regrettable since the station is a sprightly uplift to a rather dreary part of East London.

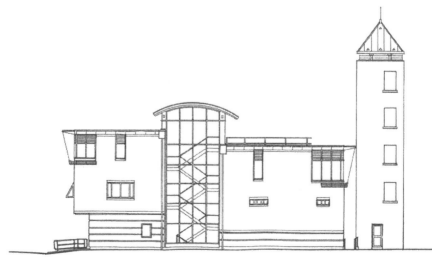

C3. Queen Mary & Westfield College Library,
1989
Mile End Road, E1
Tube: Mile End
Colin St John Wilson & Partners Ltd

C4. Queen Mary & Westfield College student accommodation, 1991
Mile End Road, E1
Tube: Mile End
MacCormac Jamieson Prichard

*Both the following buildings are excellent
examples of current architectural projects:
stringent requirements, low budgets and demands
upon the designer's inventiveness and skill.*

C3

C3. Library
Access: during term
The client's criteria called for this library called
for the accommodation of specific needs and
long term flexibility. The designer's solution
has been to seek out a strategically economic
form of adaptability, i.e. different kinds of
adaptability in different parts of the building.
The end result is an expert and efficient design.

Many of the building's features display the
Aalto-esque influences which are apparently a
concern of the practice (e.g. the lobby area, the
column treatment, the long entry staircase, blond
wood finishes, etc). This flavour continues on the
outside where the facade treatment again evokes
Aalto. The brickwork (which is a sophisticated
piece of structural design) attempts to do what the
Swedish architect Lewerentz did at St Mark's in
Stockholm; it works, but is somewhat tentative,
leaving one wondering if it was intentional or
accidental.

C4. Student accommodation
Access: during term
This piece of East End collegiate architecture is
a long terrace block facing the Grand Union
Canal and enjoying views over Mile End Park.
It provides accommodation for 72 students in
the equivalent to hotel bedrooms with en-suite
bathrooms. Kitchens and dinettes are shared –
one per stair to each of six 'houses'. The
scheme strives to provide good architecture from
its tight budget; this results in an articulation and
set of features which includes bay windows, top-
lit stairs and balconies for the top floor students.

C4

*The Informatics Teaching Laboratory on
campus by MacCormac Jamieson Prichard is
also on campus*

D. The West End

This section includes the part of London where most of the interesting new retailing interiors are (particularly around Knightsbridge).

Suggested Itinerary:

Embankment Place (D1)
Sainsbury Wing, National Gallery (D2)
Sackler Gallery (D3)
Legends (D18)
Whistles (D19)
Imagination (D6)
Stukeley Place (D5)
Brown's Club (D17)
Comyn Ching (D4)
Now and Zen (D17)

Richmond House (D9)
Queen Elizabeth II Conference Centre (D8)
Clore Gallery, Tate (D10)
Café and Whistler Restaurant, Tate (D11)
Book Shop, Tate (D12)
Crown Reach (D13)
Vauxhall Cross (D14)
Jigsaw (D20)
Stevens Building, Royal College of Art (D7)
Stephen Bull Restaurant (D16)
Brompton Cross (D21–D24)

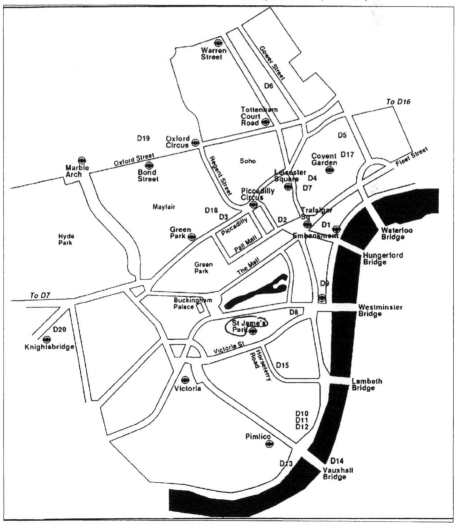

D1. Embankment Place 1991
Charing Cross Station, WC2
Tube: Embankment
Access: private, except to station and arcades
Terry Farrell & Company

Many people see Terry Farrell courting the danger of designing Hollywood sets. But he not only has an eye for dramatic architectural images, he also has a strong sensitivity toward historical issues, the community dimensions of architecture and the potential urban drama implicit in many of his projects.

Such sensibilities have informed his designs for Embankment Place, a large speculative office building utilising the air rights over Charing Cross Station. His design has tremendous presence on the river (especially at night), reinforcing memories of the Strand palaces which once lined this part of the river and still evident in the large plot sizes along the river bank. It also provides a sense of occasion along Villiers Street – where the comparatively diminutive scale of its cafes and shops contrasts with the gigantism of Farrell's design – as well as offering the drama of commuter trains ploughing in and out of the building's underbelly.

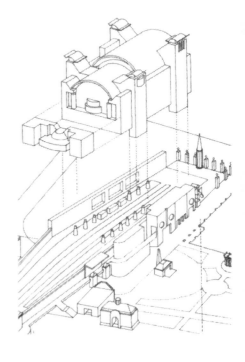

The scheme provides a host of minor, but important, urban improvements – including a direct link from Hungerford Bridge to the station, the pedestrianisation of Villiers Street), improvements to the vaulted arcades under the station, the restoration of railings to the forecourt, and restoration to the York Watergate (now attributed to Inigo Jones).

The building's floors are suspended from the arches spanning and straddling the station, bringing their structural loads down between the tracks. This provides the characteristic arching which echoes the original form of the station roof.

The station platforms have been reinterpreted as a grand interior room. Within the offices, the lobby fountain refers to a drawing by Ledoux of a river source issuing from a circular hole in a wall; there is also a vast pillar similar to that in the Kurskaya underground station in Moscow.

Walk across Hungerford Bridge to the South Bank Arts Centre for an excellent view of this building.

D2. Sainsbury Wing, National Gallery, 1990
Trafalgar Square, WC2
Tube: Charing Cross
Access: Mon-Sat 11am-6pm; Wed 11am-8pm
Venturi Rauch, Scott Brown Architects
Executive architects: Sheppard Robson

The level of design consideration shown in this building is extraordinary. But does it succeed? Opinions are sharply divided.

The building has a notable history as a problematic project suffering royal interference and sadly underfunded until sponsorship from the Sainsbury supermarket family obviated the need for commercial letting. It is the only UK building by one of the USA's most famous architects and the repository for a fabulous collection of medieval art.

The Trafalgar Square facade integrates itself by picking up the pilasters of Wilkins' building and slowly ghosting them into a new stone facade. Or perhaps it works the other way, toying with historical sequentiality so that the Wilkins facade emerges from the Venturi one like some Robert Grahame sculpture.
The upper level link between old and new avoids the cliché of a glazed connection and turns the bridge into a linked pavilion. The adjacent facade is an area of (less than successful) black glazing onto a wide main stair owing something to Alvar Aalto – yet again – and much to Pop decorative sensibilities (including a frieze of chiselled names and a series of overhead mock arches). Off the stair – at mezzanine level – is a restaurant which should have offered splendid views of Trafalgar square. It doesn't.

The architect's expertise resides elsewhere. The configuration of the gallery spaces, for example, is a skilled transfiguration of John Soane's 1826 antecedent at the Dulwich Gallery. Consideration of diagonal views of paintings, the distribution of different openings, and even air conditioning vents, have all been expertly considered. Some find the game painfully elevated and precious. Others delight in knowing a honed architectural intellect is at work.

D3. Sackler Gallery, 1991
Royal Academy of Arts, Burlington House,
Piccadilly, W1
Tube: Piccadilly
Access: public 10am–6pm
Sir Norman Foster & Partners

British designers rarely demonstrate either an
appetite or an expertise for successfully
blending the old and the new, as one finds in
some other countries. But this is exactly what
the Foster practice offers at the Sackler. Of the
few Foster projects in London, this small
conversion is possibly the most outstanding.

The three gallery spaces at the top of the
building are accessible by either a stair (with
open, glass treads) or a lift (glass, of course) in
a space which formerly held dreary narrow light
wells located between the original Burlington
House and the galleries built to the rear in 1869.
The brick and stonework has been carefully
cleaned and restored, and these spaces have
now become the fulcrum of Foster's masterplan
for making the building work.

The upper galleries follow the configuration
of the former Diploma Galleries. But the model
for the plan's extension into section is, as with
the Sainsbury and the Clore, the rooms of
Soane's Dulwich Gallery. The Sackler is a neatly
proportioned version with simple barrel-vaults,
minimal detailing, discreet handling of air-
conditioning vents, and a sensitive awareness of
scale. Electronically controlled lighting features
which allow filtered daylight or artificial light
onto the art pieces are centrally mounted.

Another key component of the architectural
scheme is the upper lobby, where light floods in
through frosted glass walls and roof. The
detailing is superb (even playful) in the manner
it addresses the difficulty of a meeting between
old and new (in this case, by employing a glass
intermediary floor panel which invariably
produces a mild insecurity as one stands upon
it). The employment of the former parapet for
classical statues helps enormously to produce
the right effect.

Only Max Gordon's Saatchi Gallery is
comparable in quality of experience, although
the difference in spatial scale (and other
matters) could hardly be more different.

D4. Comyn Ching 1984
Seven Dials, Covent Garden, WC2
Tube: Covent Garden
Access: private, but inner courtyard usually open
Terry Farrell and Company

In the days when most architectural ironmongers held vast stocks, Comyn Ching was still the one to count upon where one could find obscure fittings. They had inhabited a rabbit warren of spaces within this triangular piece of property in Covent Garden since 1723, extending everywhere and spilling out into a mess of accommodation that filled up the light well between the terraces. This was the refurbishment project Farrell took on. It shows him at his best: mending, healing and revitalising with wit, economy and inventiveness.

Farrell's strategy has been to clear out the lightwell and restore it as a courtyard; to repair and reinstate the centre sections of the three terraces; and to provide the triangular site with three new corners which proudly announce themselves and offer something to the Covent Garden of the 1980s. Uses are mixed: small apartments, office suites and retail outlets. And somewhere in there is still the (much reduced) Comyn Ching showroom.

The corners and the courtyard make up the most evident part of the architectural scheme. Each corner is different; they also poke through to become evident on the inside, in the new courtyard. This is a poorly daylit and rather dank area looking for a positive role in life, but this is part of its attraction. Another part is some strongly mannerist detailing from Farrell, particularly around the entrances, both to the court itself and to the individual units: a curious mixture of Queen Anne exuberance and Venturi's cookie-cutter profiling.

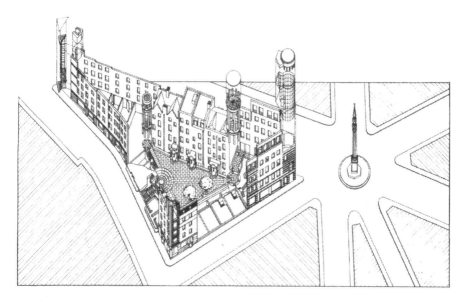

D5. Stukeley Place, 1992
20-22 Stukeley Street, Covent Garden, WC1
Tube: Covent Garden/Holborn
Access: private
Jestico + Whiles

This small conversion of an Edwardian warehouse in the eastern part of the Covent Garden area superbly milks its opportunities for architectural gamesmanship. An obvious precedent is the atrium of the much larger Imagination building; here, however, the architects have had to design on a less grand scale and for unknown occupants.

The main feature of the design is a glass covered atrium/lift lobby providing access to the tenancies on each office floor. This is a naturally ventilated space, so that windows opening on to it allow air to be vented across the offices and out through the top. The windows are, in fact, large sliding doors of frameless glass over original openings onto an existing light well.

The materials employed are render, to the walls; stainless steel details and galvanised sheet linings, sometimes perforated; glass blocks, and sheet glass – lots of it. The comparison one naturally makes is with the similar hard features of the atrium space of Hopkins' Bracken House. Whereas Hopkins' design offers material reassurance, however, one worries that Jestico and Whiles' less well-funded detailing and finishes could become a maintenance issue. Carping? Perhaps. Another reservation about this excellent building is a faceted window on the facade used to carry the street numbering. It is unnecessary, showing an eagerness to overload the building with features, just in case another opportunity doesn't come along.

But the overall impression is very positive. It is of abundant, well planned space and of deeply penetrating sunlight pouring through the roof, the glass block floors, and into the workplaces. It is economic, expert, inventive and, most importantly, considerate towards its occupants.

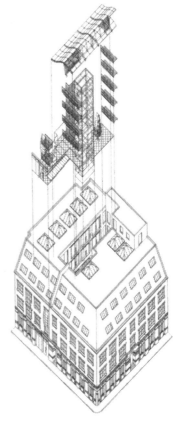

D6. Imagination, 1989
25 Store Street, WC1
Tube: Goodge Street
Access: only when public exhibitions are held
Herron Associates

Ron Herron's client for this project was a promotional firm called Imagination (their largest client has been Ford), and this building is their offices and studios.

The only hint of something special on the exterior of this Edwardian building (originally a school) is a small steel and glass canopy over the entrance – like some misplaced part of the atrium scheme for which someone had a good idea. Even the lobby (not by Herron) betrays nothing. Beyond it – where there were formerly two light wells – is the celebrated atrium. It is exhilarating as space, place, as constructional *tour de force*, and even as an exercise in artificial lighting. But the atrium is also a useful facility of indeterminate purpose – acting like some alchemical catalyst, drawing the possibility of precious things out of the dross of ordinary circumstances. It has been stage set, theatre, exhibition space, launch venue, party place, and many other things. Across it are slung artfully located bridges linking the two halves; as one looks up, people seem to theatrically appear, as if on cue.

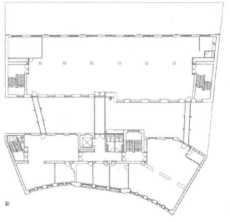

A translucent fabric enclosure wraps the long divide between the building's former north and south wings, extending itself over the lower roof of the rear wing. Everything is white, with touches of brushed stainless steel and aluminium decking. Even the toilets are lined in stainless steel (a forgivable pretence of prefabrication).

Perhaps it sounds brutal and uninviting. In fact, it is warm and refreshing, redolent with a self-assurance and concern for people. As David Allford has noted, Herron accepts, uses and disposes technology with wit, but doesn't celebrate it. He has no need of tedious rhetorical statements and his work is about as near as we get to a benchmark of unselfconscious virtuousity in British architecture.

Turn up when they have an exhibition on and you can enjoy one of the finest architectural experiences in London.

D7. Stevens building, 1992
Royal College of Art
Kensington Gore, SW7
Tube: Gloucester Road
Access: by arrangement, except to exhibition
areas
John Miller & Partners

As with most of the arts, including architecture, there is an enormous difference between an experience of varieties of playing within and around architecture, and the feeling that someone is actually producing the real thing.

This building by John Miller's practice possesses stimulating and rewarding aspects which – in places – signal that real architecture is being attended to.

The Stevens building for the painters of the RCA extends a large existing Victorian terrace house – doubling its size and providing a new mews elevation linking through to the main RCA building. The heavy-handed feeling of this mews facade is less than inspiring, but the common parts of the interior which mediate between old and new attempt to realise an inspired interior architecture which begins to blur boundaries between inside and out.

At the heart of the conversion and extension scheme is a new, galleried and toplit atrium which is used as a central focus, a gathering point and an exhibition space. The design of this white and brightly lit space design bears many influences: hints of Wagner (the post office) and the Viennese Seccession (Olbrich's building and Klimt's Beethoven frieze), Mackintosh, and Loos. Perhaps it is all rather too confined; but, above all, there is a skilled manipulation of space and light which is the essence of modern architectural sensibilities and which offers much enjoyment.

The remainder of the scheme – the studios – is more pragmatically arranged, as it should be. And one wonders: is it robust enough to withstand student onslaughts? will it bear up as Mackintosh's school in Glasgow?

D8. Queen Elizabeth II Conference Centre,
1986
Broad Sanctuary, SW1
Tube: Westminster
Access: by arrangement
Powell Moya Partnership

Powell and Moya are a well established English
practice, perhaps best known for Oxbridge
collegiate work – a note which also
characterises this building sitting opposite
Nicholas Hawksmoor's towers at Westminster
Abbey, and adjacent to the neo-gothic of
Middlesex Guildhall and the Edwardian
baroque of Central Hall. As the architects have
noted, all these buildings have sculpted facades
in stone, glass and lead – something which they
wanted to acknowledge.

The most notable features of the Centre's
exterior are a dramatic yet discreetly handled
example of structural acrobatics and an
extravagant use of lead. For structural reasons
the building has had to be constructed as two
separate halves, and this is reflected in the
planning. On a similar note, the large spans
dictated by upper level conference facilities
have generated the employment of deep beams.
These have been used to produce a dramatic
third floor cantilever which corresponds with
the roof-line of adjacent buildings. The
stepped-back penthouse levels above this hide
an inner courtyard.

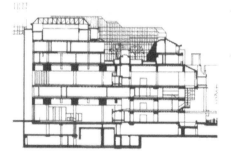

The aesthetic of the QE Centre is now
unfashionable and outside mainstream trends,
making it peculiarly idiosyncratic.
Comparisons are with Casson Conder, and
Chamberlin Powell and Bon. In the case of the
latter, there is another similarity: a rather heavy-
handed treatment of the interiors (see, for
example, the Barbican). Apart from this one
criticism, it has to be said that the Centre is a
fine building. It will be around and well
considered long after most contemporary (and
more fashionable) buildings have been
forgotten.

The Centre accommodates an auditorium
for 1000 people; four variously sized rooms to
seat another 500, a committee room for 200,
offices for delegates, bars, restaurants, etc.

D9. Richmond House, 1987
Department of Health, Whitehall, SW1
Tube: Westminster
Access: private
Whitfield and Partners

Like the QE II Conference centre, this building
falls into an anachronistic category of aesthetic
concerns which underlies prevailing
architectural tastes, but popping up now and
then: something quintessentially English,
vaguely collegiate, and simultaneously offering
historical reassurance, yet somehow still
modern. Arguably, it is an appropriate
architectural style for Whitehall and, although
unfashionable, quietly remains in accord with
its own standards of excellence. Other
buildings exhibiting these qualities include the
QE II Conference Centre (Powell and Moya)
and 85 London Wall (Casson Conder).

Whitfield's building for the Department
of Health self-consciously acknowledges its
Norman Shaw neighbour, New Scotland Yard
(1890): rich red brickwork and strips of stone.
Other materials are ash and lead. The windows
over the forecourt (behind them is the
Reception Room; immediately in front is
Lutyens' Cenotaph) are distinctly Jacobean in
flavour .

But this is not dressing up, not the
miming of thin post-modernism – it is the real
thing, done very seriously and without irony.

*A similar building by Whitfield can be
found in Rampayne Street, SW1 (the
Metropolitan Police Office, 1982). This rather
bulky building is near Darbourne and Darke's
excellent Lillington Gardens housing project of
1972.*

Tate Gallery

D10. Clore Gallery, 1986
Millbank, SW1
Tube: Pimlico
Stirling Wilford & Associates

D11. Restaurants, 1984
Millbank, SW1
Tube: Pimlico
Jeremy & Fenella Dixon

D12. Bookshop, 1991
Millbank, SW1
Tube: Pimlico
John Miller + Partners

D10

D10. Clore Gallery
Access: Mon-Sat 10am–5.50pm; Sun
2pm–5.50pm

Like the Sackler and the Sainsbury – London's
other public art galleries built in the 1980s – the
Clore is a product of private rather than state
patronage. It can hardly be said to have won
people's hearts and minds, but we believe it is
one of the few buildings of the period likely to
make many friends in the long term.

The gallery is a skilled extension to Smith's
1897 edifice (also sponsored by a private patron,
the sugar magnate Sir Henry Tate). It simply
integrates itself as a part of the overall site
composition, yet remains clearly a discrete
entity in its own right. Its landscaped forecourt
establishes a quiet note (contrasting with Smith's
somewhat bombastic building) and constitutes
the gallery as a pavilion in an English garden.

In a manner comparable with Venturi's
work on the Sainsbury Wing, Stirling employs
the geometries of his predecessor, picking up its
classical motifs where new and old join
together, then quickly erodes their presence,
allowing his own architecture to take over
(although a vestige of Smith remains in the
underlying horizontal partitioning of the
facade). At the other end, he picks up the
geometries and materials of the corner villa and
establishes a similar transmutation and
integration (the brickwork, for example, appears
to leap the gap and insinuate itself into the
Stirling Wilford building).

As ever, the jokiness is there: the irritating
arid green, the missing stone in the base (at the
junction with Smith's building), and brickwork
which appears to hang without support.

D10

D11

55

Arrangements within the gallery contrast with a different kind of expertise exercised by Venturi Scott Brown at the Sainsbury. The comfortable enfilade rooms of the first floor are enhanced by the inclusion of some simple pieces of peripheral place-making and architectural gamesmanship, e.g. the balcony to the stair overlooking the first room, and the delightfully contrived oriel which provides a contemplative retreat and view over the entry court.

Comparisons should be made by visits to the Sackler, the Whitechapel, the Saatchi, the Sainsbury (and perhaps the paradigm of gallery spaces to which some of these refer: John Soane's Dulwich Picture Gallery).

D11. Restaurants
D12. Bookshop
Access: Mon–Sat 10am–5.50pm;
Sun 2pm–5.50pm
Visitors to the Clore should also see the restored spatial grandeur of the 1937 sculpture gallery; Jeremy & Fenella Dixon's basement coffee shop and their Whistler Restaurant (its strikingly lit mural is by Rex Whistler); and John Miller's Nomura Gallery and Tate Shop.

D12

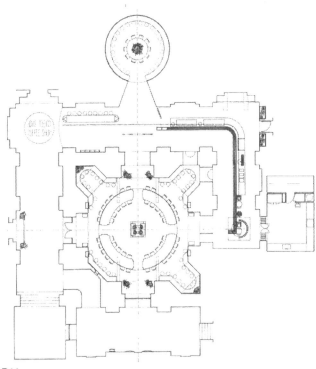

D11

D13. Crown Reach, 1984
Grosvenor Road, SW1
Tube: Pimlico
Access: private
Nicholas Lacey, Jobst and Partners

Crown Reach achieved high profile as a competition with 462 entrants won by Nicholas Lacey. For a long time it was the only significant piece of modern architecture along this stretch of river. Then the Clore and Vauxhall Cross became its neighbours.

The scheme attempts to reconcile conflicting considerations: to grasp the benefits of a river edge location; to turn its back to the noisy main road along the embankment; to provide a public walkway along the river; to avoid building an esplanade which might separate the buildings from the river; and to offer a protective environment.

The design sweeps around from a low mid-point to its high ends in order to provide residents with clear views both up and down river. The two ends simultaneously reach out to the river, creating arcades over the walkway. The centre is pulled back to provide a sheltered open space into which apartments look.

It is a design which mixes the best of 1970s high-density / low-rise thinking with a verve then uncommon in housing.

Unfortunately, the walkway is yet another well-meaning but inaccessible gesture which goes from nowhere to nowhere. It is a very private and introverted development. It is also a rather sombre scheme which has none of the lightness of touch of the Heron Quays scheme.

The scheme has some 60 apartments, together with offices and studios.

D14. Vauxhall Cross 1992
Albert Embankment, SE1
Tube: Vauxhall
Access: private
Terry Farrell and Company

Surrounded by comment and rumour, Vauxhall Cross is certainly a bizarre scheme. The developers were supposedly saved from financial difficulty by a Government offer to use the building for MI6; there followed the omission of luxury apartments and a rapid change of use. Or was it the other way around? Wilder rumour even hints at an underground fast exit route from Whitehall through the site. Whatever, the secret service now has splendid river terraces with fountains (actually a security moat) and an array of too-perfect-to be-true conical trees (rumoured by the unkind, of course, to be plastic).

Although the striking green glass and cream concrete massing defies a simple interpretation of inner organisation, the architectural references appear to come from New York of the 1920s and 1930s when capitalism wore broad shoulder pads, sported a moderne guise and strutted its stepped-back stuff. This is the Rockefeller Center, Holabird and Root, Raymond Hood, Bertram Goodhue and Hugh Ferri; there is even a hint of early Frank Lloyd Wright in LA.

Some see this building as possibly Farrell's most controlled and mature building – a rich diet, certainly, but not a cacophony of rhetorical **features, nor without the unselfconscious virtuosity which can uplift and excite. But it is**

undoubtedly too Gotham City for the taste of many. Farrell's many critics and opponents – who include the neo-classicists as well as the hi-tech camp – would call it a nightmare: a secret service fortress, provided by a private speculator, designed by an avowed populist, and sited on a most prominent river location. Indubitably, it is a bizarre phenomenon. But visit it, throw away architectural politics and make up your own mind.

D15. Channel Four
Horseferry Road, SW1
Tube: St James's Park
Access: private
Richard Rogers & Partners

The Channel Four building in Victoria makes an interesting contrast with two other recent media projects: Foster's cool and patrician exercise for ITN and Farrell's hot and populist TV-AM building in Camden. Channel Four is different to both. As a significant London building from the Rogers practice it is also markedly different in character to Lloyds and Reuters, exhibiting some of the substantiality and quality of Hopkins' work on the old Financial Times building and just a hint of the flamboyance and structural acrobatics invariably employed by Grimshaw. It stands out among the social housing and bland civil service buildings characterizing this part of Victoria.

D14

D15

Central interiors

There are more than a few differences between a John Lewis department store and a Nigel Coates clothes shop, and it is more the latter end of the interior spectrum that interests us in this section. Here, interiors are high on added value and low on relevance to anything other than current fashions.

Life-cycles can be brutally short; the investment is deliberately short-term. The name of the game is to push the conversation, to be at the front-edge, to have a finger on the pulse of frivolity, elegance or both. It is also to flaunt the eternal, relentless return of the commodity as something fresh and new – to believe it is new and to live out that belief. The agenda is to reassure that, yes, nothing matters but a knowing participation in the rituals of discrimination and consumption. As high art, the pretence must be maintained that commerce is pertinent but incidental.

D16

Two restaurants

D16. Stephen Bull Restaurant, 1992
St. John Street, EC1
Tube: Barbican
Allies and Morrison

D17. Now and Zen, 1991
4a Upper St Martin's Lane, WC2
Tube: Leicester Square
Rick Mather Architects

D16. Stephen Bull Restaurant
Access: normal restaurant hours
Allies and Morrison's sentiments are at odds with the theatrical place-making often demanded of interior designers. As Bob Allies has commented, 'We've avoided doing things that are driven by fashion.' All of which makes this restaurant the more remarkable. It strives to offer substantiality and to employ an unadorned language of space, light and simple forms – plus some strong colouring demanded by the client.

Bull's demonstrates a consistent exploration of layered and interpenetrating rectangular components and volumes affecting the architectural detail as well as the fundamental *parti*. You see it in the contrived wall layering; the volumes of entry passage, main restaurant and suspended mezzanine; in the strong patches of wall colouring; in the metalwork details of the security gate (becoming an A+M trademark) and the slim flatness of the handrailing. Minimalism is offered as considered refinement rather than a reductive end in itself.

D17. Now and Zen

Access: restaurant hours

Rick Mather has recently achieved much
attention with a series of up-market Chinese
restaurants each of which attempts to strip away
the cultural associations of the type. The first –
ZeNW3, in Hampstead village – has many of
the features developed in later versions (*Zen
Central, Mayfair; Ma & Pa, High Road N20*).

The Zen in St. Martin's has a large glass
frontage incorporating an all glass revolving
door (no steel framing at all). In front of this is
an area of clear glass paving guaranteed to
disturb many visitors. Inside, every effort has
been made to link the spaces of the basement,
ground floor and mezzanine. An outstanding
feature is a glass dragon waterfall of glass
bowls that start at the ceiling and fall down to
the basement. The aesthetic is clean, lively and
sparkling. As Mather says, 'There is not a dull
table in the place'.

D17

D18. Legends, 1987

29 Old Burlington Street, W1
Tube: Green Park
Access: lunchtime restaurant Monday to Friday;
evenings is a club (no membership required).

This club is by Eva Jiricna, an
engineer/architect by training who is associated
with a penchant for the hi-tech. But the
interiors she designs mix hard edge toughness
and rigour with refinement and subtlety.

As in so many of Jiricna's projects, this
club includes stunning hi-tech stairs as the most
prominent feature of the architectural tableaux
she assembles. She has realised a whole series
of these stainless steel and glass beasts across
central London, all of which can be tracked
down and admired.

D18

Two disparate shops

D19. Whistles, 1992
12 St Christopher's Place , W1
Tube: Bond Street
Stanton Williams

D20. Jigsaw, 1991
31 Brompton Road, SW3
Tube: Knightsbridge
Branson Coates

D19

D19. Whistles
Access: normal shop hours
This Stanton Williams shop for Whistles has a
characteristically cool and refined quality. The
palette of materials is simple; but the intriguing
thing about Stanton Williams' work is the
manner in which they make the elements of their
designs work to strong architectural effect.

*Other work includes the Issey Miyake shop
in Brompton Road (see below); the Kriston
Laundry at 307 Kings Road, SW3; and the
Classic FM radio station at 24 Oval Road, NW1.*

D20. Jigsaw
Access: normal shop hours
Branson Coates characterise their
designs as 21st century Arts and
Crafts. Contemporary mannerism
might be more apt. At
Knightsbridge, for example, 'the
double height glass facade allows a
tantalising glimpse into the main
upper salon. The approach across
the stone paved ground floor and
up the sweeping open central
staircase is reflected in a wall of
mirror – beyond that, the soft grey

> **Alan Stanton's
> contemporary best:**
> • Lloyd's of London
> • Financial Times, Isle
>   of Dogs
> • Kenzo, Brownlow
>   Mews
> • Foster's building,
>   Stockley Park
> • The Brittanic House
>   conversion
> • Bracken House

greens, a further vista of blues and hot golds
upstairs. As you go up the curved terrazzo
stairway a huge chandelier spirals down.
Lapping the upper steps a great oval carpet wraps
the well, and at the room's periphery the
sundrenched Jigsaw colours are scattered up the
wall above the clothes – in a spectacular
commissioned wall painting by the artist Stuart
Helm. Noteworthy details include Nigel Coates'
tongue armchairs.' (BC) So there.

*Other work includes Jigsaw shops in
Kensington High Street, Kings Road and St
Christopher's Place; a Katherine Hammnett
shop in Sloane Street and a jewellery shop in
Burlington Gardens.*

D20

Four at Brompton Cross

D21. Joseph, 1988
77 Fulham Road SW3
Tube: South Kensington
Eva Jiricna Architects

D22. Joe's Café, 1986
Draycott Avenue SW3
Tube: South Kensington
Eva Jiricna Architects

D23. Issey Miyake
270 Brompton Road SW3 2AN
Tube: South Kensington
Stanton Williams

D24. Wilson & Gough, 1992
106 Draycott Avenue SW3
Tube: South Kensington
David Chipperfield

Brompton Cross is an intersection around which a number of up-market retail outlets have gathered.

D21. Joseph
D22. Joe's Café
Access: normal shop hours
Joseph and Joe's Café are both typical of Eva Jiricna's work (see earlier).

D23. Issey Miyake
Access: normal shop hours
The Issey Miyake (women's) shop is the last remaining of two designed by Stanton Williams. It is quite special.

D24. Wilson & Gough
Access: normal shop hours
David Chipperfield's work is informed by a search for basic qualities transcending stylistic issues. In his Wilson and Gough crafts shop the strategy was to conceal elements of structure within a 'cabinet wall' running through the middle of the shop; this provides the shop with a circular route.

D21

D22

D23

D24

E. Heading north

This section covers five areas of north London:
- *West of Regent's Park (Marylebone and Paddington), but including the Park itself.*
- *Around Kings Cross.*
- *East of Regent's Park (Camden and Kentish Town).*
- *Around Hampstead Heath.*
- *Out beyond, i.e. further out from central London to areas such as Walthamstow and, even, Epping.*

Suggested Itinerary:
Michael Hopkins' office (E3)
Lisson / Bell Street galleries (E4)
Lisson Grove offices (E5)
Ashmill Street housing (E7)
Clifton Nursery (E8)

West of Regent's Park: Marylebone and Paddington

On the whole, this area is far more affluent than the following section – the other side of Regent's Park. On the west side we have Quinlan Terry's villas for the rich, a new stand for Middlesex cricket fans at Lords, and an art gallery for one of the Saatchi brothers. Even the welfare housing we cite has a classy overtone.

Lanark Road housing (E9)
Saatchi Gallery (E6)
The Mound Stand (E2)
Regent's Park villas (E1)
St Mark's Road housing (E10)
Lancaster Road offices (E11)

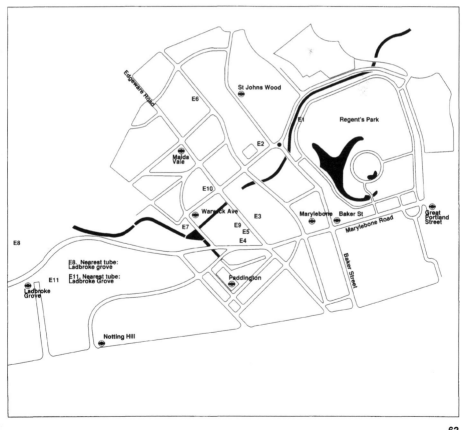

E1. Regent's Park villas, 1992
Outer Circle, North Regents Park, NW1
Tube: Baker Street/St. John's Wood
Access: private
Erith and Terry

Quinlan Terry is an incongruous architect in a
faithless age. His classicism has the serious
overtones of 18th-century Palladianism,
conscious of an educated and God-fearing
man's duties in the public realm to display
virtue and exercise decorum. Critics who carp
at his correctness sometimes betray, one
suspects, the envy of people with a lesser self-
conviction. You'll either intensely enjoy or hate
these sumptuous, electronically equipped dream
homes for the rich.

Architecturally, the three villas (there are
five planned) make little sense outside the Nash
tradition of detached villas that were planned
for the Park and are evident at Park Village.
(Perhaps they also make little sense outside a
more contemporary tradition evident in Bishop's
Avenue – the Millionaire's Row of north
London, where a less erudite version of the neo-
classical detached villa has manifest itself.) But
these villas are more Palladian than the informal
Tuscan *villa rustica* format preferred by Nash at
Park Village. They are also without leanings
toward the picturesque of *cottages ornés*.
Instead, their symmetrical playfulness is of a
very serious nature. The outer form wears a
smile, but it is all terribly self-conscious and
well mannered. Naughty, in fact. One suspects
that the inner spirit is rather po-faced.

Each villa adopts a different theme:
Gothick, Veneto, and Ionic. Continuities are
provided by scale, underlying configuration and
a simple language of materials (principally
Portland stone and render).

*Two other Erith and Terry buildings to
visit are at Richmond riverside (offices and
shops), and Dufours Place, Soho (offices and
flats).*

64

E2. Mound Stand, 1991
Lord's Cricket Ground, St John's Wood, NW8
Tube: St John's Wood
Access: tours by arrangement
Michael Hopkins and Partners

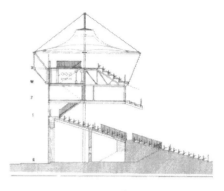

Hopkins has become one of the more interesting
of British architects, consistently offering a
'thick' architecture rich in consideration and
expert in execution. The Mound Stand is a
good example.

In essence, Hopkins' team has retained the
original lower-level terrace and designed new
facilities – a superstructure incorporating a new
upper terrace, a row of private rooms and
viewing boxes, and a top terrace with
refreshment bars. All this is on a relatively
small number of steel columns which offer little
visual obstruction.

The whole edifice floats above the original
terracing and is tied back to massive brick
arches along the street facade. Six of the latter
are original – extended to 27 by Hopkins in an
authentic loadbearing construction.

The superstructure is a vertically layered
concept, at the heart of which is a massive steel
truss. Below it are the private boxes; slung
beneath them is a new terrace; above it is the
upper terrace and, above that, the tensile fabric
roof (of pvc). Since the stand is only used for a
few weeks in the year, the construction is
simple and straightforward (no heating,
insulation, etc).

It is the fabric roof which provides the
Mound Stand with its singularly appropriate
image. It has festive and summery associations:
marquees, yachts and the like. One can laze
about up here, bathing in the diffused light
while sipping a drink from the bar watching
**Middlesex perform on the carpet of green out
front and listening to the crack of leather on
willow.**

*Just round the corner, in Lodge Road, is an
office building designed by Michael Hopkins for
IBM.*

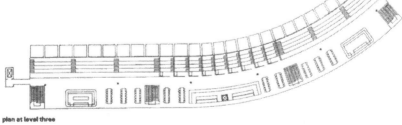

plan at level three

Three in Lisson Grove

E3. Michael Hopkins' office, 1985
27 Broadley Terrace, NW1
Tube: Marylebone/Edgware
Michael Hopkins and Partners

E4. Lisson/Bell Street galleries, 1991
52 Bell Street, NW8
Tube: Marylebone/Edgware
Tony Fretton Architects

E5. Lisson Grove offices and flats, 1990
31-35 Lisson Grove NW8
Tube: Marylebone/Edgware
Trevor Horne Architects

E3

E3. Michael Hopkins' office
Access: private
This is an unexpected building to find in
Marylebone: a Hopkins-designed prefabricated
building. Its novelty is its sophistication – in
the engineering and a design which utilises the
same double-walled, insulated cladding panels
for walls and roof. Here, Hopkins has
discreetly squeezed the Patera unit on to a
small site opposite a Victorian school. Inside is
one large, open volume with a mezzanine.

E4. Lisson/Bell Street galleries
Access: normal gallery hours
This is actually two merged galleries. The first,
in Lisson Street, is a conversion completed a
few years ago by Fretton; the second has taken
an empty site around the corner, in Bell Street.
The two link together behind the corner
junction of the two streets, providing an L plan.

Fretton has provided his art dealer client
with a minimal aesthetic of white walls,
screeded floors, maple flooring, few details,
and lots of dramatic toplighting – the kind of
place considered to be required by the
international art scene. Fretton describes it as
'the making of romantic spaces from the bare
facts of their existence.' The design is very
adaptable and robust: windows come out,
handrailing can be dismantled – all to facilitate
all kinds of art – the large, awkward, and the
rest.

The Bell Street facade is a carefully
composed piece which floats a rendered wall
above large sliding glass doors. At the upper
level are wooden loading doors. The top floor
is a small apartment.

E4

E5. Lisson Grove offices and flats

Access: private

This small development is a conversion of three plots in a late Georgian terrace in Lisson Grove. It includes the corner junction with Bell Street where the architect has taken the opportunity offered by conversion work to provide a modernist reinterpretation. The three sites are redefined as two buildings, providing shops, apartments and offices; the facade of each block is carefully articulated.

The corner block is a stark facade of white render, its window treatment emphasising the corner's importance. It is, in fact, an adaptation of a 1960s building on the site which has been reordered and given an additional storey. The adjacent block seeks to align itself with existing terrace features while maintaining its own individual and modernist character. The parapet, for example, lines through with three of the lower buildings along the terrace; above it are large dormers with projecting eaves which line through with the eaves of the new corner roof line.

The scheme is carefully and sensitively considered. The planners, however, were not in sympathy and Horne had to fight a not unusual battle to get planning permission.

This is an interesting area to wander around, especially for second hand bookshops.

E6. Saatchi Gallery, 1985
98A Boundary Road, NW8
Tube: Swiss Cottage
Access: Fridays and Saturdays, 12am-6pm
Max Gordon

This is one of the finest pieces of architecture in London. In few other works does one get such a delightful sense of simple space and light – it is exhilarating just to watch people move about the spaces. Few art works can compare with this magical architectural art manufactured between the building and its visitors. This experience is greatly enhanced by the hanging policy of the gallery: very few works, spread around the vastness of the late Gordon's panoramic scheme. It is a superb place.

The building was originally an industrial shed of the most utilitarian sort – land-locked, top-lit by north-lights, and of an odd configuration. Just as Frank Gehry was to do at the Temporary Contemporary in Los Angeles, Gordon accepted what existed and converted it in a most direct, economical and simple way. There are neither fancy maple floors or expensive Erco light fittings, no cloth walls or expensive Danish door furniture, no cafe or cultural accoutrements – just a marvellous, stripped sense of space and place – toplit, white walls, painted concrete floor – so appropriate to its purpose and so enjoyable in itself.

On a planning level, Gordon has organised storage, offices, toilets and the like as intermediary and boundary servant spaces defining the main gallery spaces themselves.

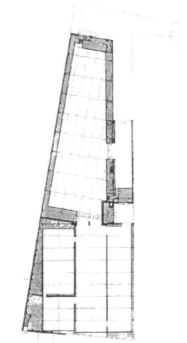

There is a disjuncture between this planning and the original perimeter, offering a kind of informal *poche* space which is contradicted at the upper level by the way one can read the roof-lights sailing over the partitions to the original outer wall. The designer is in total control – exploiting what he finds, but articulating a manifest separateness within the original shell. The detailing searches for immediacy, for a discreetness and reticence which underscores the importance of space and light in themselves.

Four by Jeremy Dixon
(E7 with BDP, E9 and E10 with Fenella Dixon)

E7. Ashmill Street housing, 1984
Ashmill Street, Marylebone, NW8
Tube: Edgeware Road

E8. Clifton Nursery, 1985
Clifton Villas, Warwick Avenue, W9
Tube: Warwick Avenue

E9. Lanark Road housing, 1983
171–201 Lanark Road W9
Tube: Warwick Avenue

E10. St Mark's Road housing, 1980
103-105 St. Mark's Road, W10
Tube: Ladbroke Grove

These three projects are good illustrations of contexturalist concerns countering the homogenising influences underlying post-modern culture. They demonstrate attempts to establish a rationale for designing architecture which is both prompted by and rooted in regional cultural traditions. To the Dixons this means an urbane tradition of London streets, terraces and villas which have characterised the city ever since the development of Georgian London . Their aim is to provide an architecture with significances and meanings reaching toward some statement which can be claimed to carry a note of authenticity.

E7

E7. Ashmill Street housing
Access: private
This is a terraced scheme small two-storey maisonettes above basement apartments. The general form follows the traditional pattern of semi-basement floors set at a half level below the street; the maisonettes are accessed by a set of steel steps. The key feature of the terrace is a vertical emphasis provided by tall and narrow triangular windows. This device is also used at Compass Point, in the Isle of Dogs.

E8

E8. Clifton Nursery

Access: normal shop hours

Clifton Nursery is a small up-market gardening centre in Little Venice – a dense, delightful place aimed toward inspiring you to buy and plant.

The Dixon scheme is a number of elements intended to enhance the presentation of the nurseries, but especially a new shop for seeds, books, tools, etc. Like the Ark, it has a copper roof reluctant to adopt a green patina. Its other predominant material is oak, structured as a simple roof over a pergola. The overhanging gable effect is very similar to what Inigo Jones achieved with St Paul's in Covent Garden.

E9

E9. Lanark Road housing

Access: private

In contrast to St Mark's, the Lanark Road project adopts the villa form, prevalent in London since the late 18th century.

The project comprises five units containing 35 low-cost apartments, constructed as unfinished shells for completion by the tenants. Each group of seven apartments enjoys its participation in a single villa unit – simple interiors and a strong image for the frontage (but one avoiding the anonymity of a large block). Access is between the units.

E10. St Mark's Road housing

Access: private

The St Mark's Road project of 44 dwellings is prompted by the form of Victorian terraces surrounding the site. The designers describe it as rather like the Queen Anne style in being 'eclecticism with an artistic eye'.

E10

Each of the twelve units is, in fact, two narrow town houses over apartments, the latter at a lower half-level in the traditional manner of London terraces. Unlike other London terraces, however, these are set at an angle to the street to maintain privacy and, according to the designers, support a means of traversing the angled corner of the site.

E11. Lancaster Road offices, 1991
87 Lancaster Road, W11
Tube: Ladbroke
Access: private
Munkenbeck and Marshall

This is a medium-size infill block of offices near Portobello Road. Its developer-client, as for Rick Mather's Pennington Road and M+M's office building in Wandsworth (Jessica Square), was the late Michael Baumgarten, an architect who was formerly a partner of Julyan Wickham (it's an incestuous world). This common denominator shows through all three developments.

The design of Lancaster Road articulates a number of layered elements, illustrating current architectural preoccupations to provide imagery and novelty as well as answer the design brief.

The features include the flat, rendered facade; a four storey bay window to the street ('The front is really a waffle iron with square windows poked in it', as the architects put it), which links into the access steps and an outreaching wall; the separate stair and lift cores; an upward curving roof to the penthouse office suite; and a long curving wall whose sweep penetrates the plan and affects the other elements. The curved wall sweeping through the plan – which is actually split and slid sideways at a crucial plan location, where the stair and lift lobby is created – helps to create a number of distinctly different sub-tenancies, each of which has its own identity within the framework of the whole.

The building is an excellent example of good 'designer-speculative' architecture. It makes little sense if read only architecturally, or simply as a developer's equation of sub-lettable units and plot maximisation. Bring these considerations together, and one has a meaningful reading of the building. Well, almost. You also have to add pure design motivation: 'It's an ode to Rietveld's Schroeder House', comments Marshall in the typically erudite but slightly tongue-in-cheek manner which has brought designers, developer and users together in this creative dialogue.

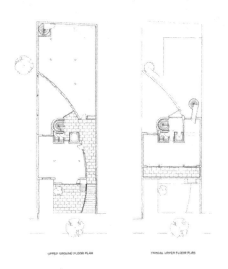

UPPER GROUND FLOOR PLAN   TYPICAL UPPER FLOOR PLAN

Around King's Cross
E12–E18

King's Cross still awaits its moment. Few sites have more potential, and development plans (master-planned by Norman Foster) have been approved. Meanwhile there is a recession, an over-supply of office space and indecision regarding the Channel terminal.

South and north of the station are entirely different in character, but the whole area is easily walkable. The projects listed as Four in Pentonville refer to where the Regent's Canal meets Caledonian Road – an area somewhat independent of the King's Cross influence. The immense British Library has a life all of its own, but it is a welcome addition to the area; meanwhile, one awaits renewal of proposals for the adjacent St Pancras Station.

East and north of Regents Park: Camden and Kentish Towns
E19–E26

To the east and north of Regent's Park is Camden Town and Kentish Town, leading up to Hampstead and Highgate (the following section).

Camden – described in 1850 as thickly inhabited by professional men – has become a prime location for architects to live and practice. It used to be a quiet country area for Londoners to resort to until development began in 1791 and brought with it the Regent's Canal, warehousing and associated industries. Then came the railways and the rail yards, and it was brought to a poorer standing.

Kentish Town was similarly a rural retreat until development started at the end of the eighteenth century and, especially, after 1840. The coming of the railways ousted the middle classes and transformed the area.

In this cultural melting pot (of professionals, and Greek and Irish immigrants), are a number of interesting recent buildings, supplementing a large body of 1970s housing estates designed by a local authority architects' department which, at the time, set standards that were the envy of the profession.

Suggested Itinerary:
ITN (E12)
British Library (E13)
Grimaldi Park House (E14)
Bridge Wharf (E15)
Regent's Wharf (E16)
Porters South (E17)
Porters North (E18)

Suggested Itinerary:
TV-AM (E19)
Sainsbury supermarket (E20)
Two houses by David Wild (E22)
Agar Studios (E21)
Bruges Place (E24)
Crowndale Centre (E25)
Jazz Café (E23)
One Off Studio (E26)

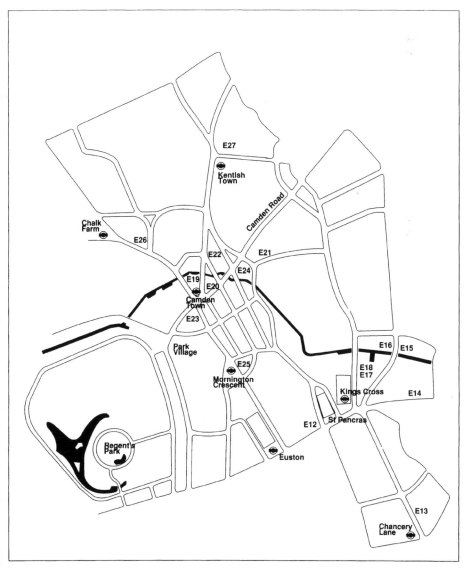

E12. ITN, 1990
200 Grays Inn Road, WC1
Tube: Chancery Lane
Access: Groups only, by appointment
Sir Norman Foster and Partners

There are few buildings by Foster in London and one naturally gives attention to whatever his practice has realised. This building is clearly an intelligent piece of design, but appears curiously thin and shallow rather than thick and rich. It's as if the design got little further than a diagram and the majority of the subsequent effort was applied to designing a simple exterior cladding system (nonetheless, a characteristically sophisticated and very elegant feature).

A galleried central atrium which lies within the heart of the building extends down into a basement space created by the site's former occupants, a newspaper printing works. Its rather disappointing effect is bravely challenged by a suspended sculptural piece designed by Ben Johnson, struggling to lend vigour to an otherwise artless place.

To be fair, the Foster office originally desired to enliven matters. They attempted to overcome the predilection of agencies similar to ITN (Reuters, in Dockland, is a good example) to withdraw from the public realm by facilitating interaction with the public by means of devices such as giant electronic displays in the entrance foyer, thus making ITN a truly public building. However, a mix of planning opposition and a mean budget took their toll. The result is an impression of potential unfulfilled. But it is still a building above average.

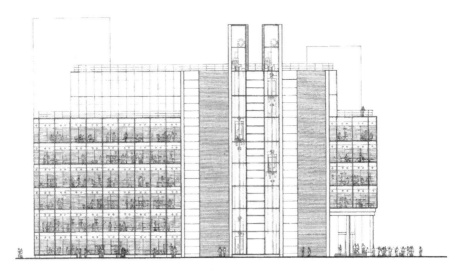

E13. British Library, 1993 (Phase 1)
Euston Road, NW1
Tube: King's Cross
Access: public
Colin St John Wilson & Partners Ltd

It's been a long time coming. What has been
realised has four significant features: it is large
(although a further stage is to come, and even
that has been truncated); it provides a much
needed new urban square as a forecourt; it has a
fine, Aalto-esque interior; and it has a rather
curious exterior which appears to have left
something out between the concept of the
massing and the few evident details (which
include some less than satisfactory features, e.g.
the detailing of solar shading devices).

The statistics are as large as the building's
roof: 3000 readers, 3000 staff, 112,500sq. m,
£450m. to build, and so on. Books are stored
below ground in three basements. Other
facilities include reading rooms, exhibition
galleries, photographic labs, offices, seminar
rooms, a publications shop, a conference centre,
etc.

The comparatively lively aesthetic of the
interiors is in striking contrast to the dull red of
the outside, which ostensibly matches Gilbert
Scott's brickwork at St Pancras, opposite.
Access from the street is through a railed and
landscaped forecourt set apart from the traffic
of Euston Road.

The interiors will include a six-storey
tower for the King's Library which is
reminiscent of Gordon Bunshaft's rare books
library at Yale: a tall, glass encased and air-
conditioned box within the external envelope of
the building. This is now a focal point of the
interiors, which otherwise employ an Alvar
Aalto theme taking one back to the roots of a
design initiated some twenty years ago, when
Aalto was still a major influence of that
generation of British architects. It also touches
upon the stamina of the architects in working on
this complex building and its changing brief for
so long.

Also see Wilson's Queen Mary &
Westfield College Library in the East End.

E14. Grimaldi Park House, 1990
Grimaldi Park, Pentonville Road, N1
Tube: King's Cross
Access: private
Allies and Morrison

This is both an odd building and an expertly
handled commission. It is a product of the
Church Commissioners' and local planners'
insistence that any new building should respect
the memory of the 1787 church formerly on the
site (demolished in 1981).

One can be sympathetic to the underlying
intent. But there is a bizarre note in the
condition that the new building – designed as a
corporate furniture showroom and offices –
should have the same general massing,
complete with pediment and steeple.

Not to be beaten, Allies and Morrison
responded with an urbane inventiveness which
identified the church facade and the notion of a
pavilion in a landscaped setting as key features
of the design.

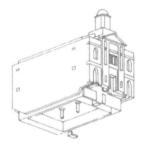

The initial concept of the facade was to
sever it from the body of the offices, and this is
still evident in the completed building (a feature
attempted again in the practice's work in
Ashland Place, Marylebone, for example).
Behind the brick wrap of the outer skin a simple
white inner realm peeks through.

But it is the considered detailing which
suggests that the designers possess expertise
and artfulness. It quietly signals that this is a
building to examine closely: that this is real
architecture being practised, even if the
architects are mildly shy about the final result.
Look, for example, at the main entrance door,
including the platform and handrail. Or the
treatment of the fenestration and how the
interior lobby has been dealt with.

*Other London work by Allies and
Morrison includes Bull's Restaurant in
Clerkenwell, Ashland Place off Paddington
Street, and the Clove Building behind the
Design Museum.*

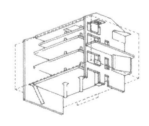

E15. Bridge Wharf, 1988
Caledonian Road, N1
Tube: King's Cross
Chassay Wright

E16. Regent's Wharf, 1991
All Saints Street, N1
Tube: King's Cross
Rock Townsend

E17. Porters South, 1990
4 Crinan Street N1
Tube: King's Cross
Fitch RS

E18. Porters North, 1988
8 Crinan Street, N1
Tube: King's Cross
DEGW

This is warehouse country – a place at the junction of railways and canals. By now it should have been enjoying booming property values and redevelopment resulting from Norman Foster's design for the area north of King's Cross station. However, his proposals for what would have been London's most significant area of redevelopment since Broadgate (in the City) have been curtailed by the recession.

E15

E15. Bridge Wharf
Access: private
This development is not dissimilar in aim to that of Jestico and Whiles at Bruges Place. It consists of live-work studios arranged around access courtyards next to the canal, and two Grade II listed Georgian buildings refurbished as offices. The complex is a welcome addition to the area.

E16. Regent's Wharf
Access: private
This is a large canalside complex of offices and studios comprising fourteen buildings totalling some 239,000sq.ft. The architect's challenge was to produce a viable scheme for refurbishing four existing warehouses, a 'new build facsimile of a locally-listed building', and nine new buildings.

Regent's is less pompous, more calm and self-assured than the practice's rampantly post-modernist work on another large office complex at the Angel, Islington. At Regent's, there is a hint of Allies and Morrison's fenestration at Grimaldi Park House; and the large copper-clad

E16

protrusions possibly extend from the practice's work with Ralph Erskine on the Ark (similar Scandinavian overtones are evident in the large areas of timber cladding conjoined with white painted steelwork within the internal courtyard).

E17. Porters South
E18. Porters North

Access: by appointment

These are adjacent warehouse conversions overlooking Battlebridge Basin, within Regent's canal, occupied by rival design practices.

Both firms have retained the robust character of the original buildings, but it is Fitch who have made the most dramatic internal interventions. They introduce an entirely new geometry cutting across internal masonry walls to dramatically create top-lit visual links between entrance lobby and canal basin at the rear. A space at the basin side is treated as a concourse focusing shared activities – dining, conference rooms, etc. Similar interventions create links between floors, producing a spatial complexity.

Such complexity has been avoided by DEGW, who employ a more simple space planner's rationale to their conversion. Whereas Fitch fracture the deep space of the building with new openings, DEGW have accepted the depth and use it to lend a calm spacious quality to their offices. Highlights are also more discreet and less rhetorical.

E17

E18

E18

E19. TV-AM, 1982
Hawley Crescent, NW1
Tube: Camden Town
Access: private
Terry Farrell and Company

This conversion of a former garage into studios
for a breakfast television station was perfect for
Farrell, allowing him to amply exercise his
skills as an inventive refurbishment architect
and indulge his greatest love: place-making.
This is classic Farrell – a design which is both
intellectually rich and populist. Since the loss
of TV-AM's licence a question mark hangs over
the building's future.

Outside, the building establishes a strong
presence. Its billboard design is prompted by
an association of breakfast TV and the sunrise:
a new, sweeping blank facade is articulated by
coloured bands – starting off red and becoming
yellow – arising from a dark grey base. This is
supplemented by large, cookie-cutter signage
on the corners and a huge, open-framed steel
arch with an abstracted keystone, outlined in
neon and evoking a rising sun. This acts as the
gateway to a small entry court. On the canal
side new windows, bright colouring and,
especially, large eggs in egg-cups adorning the
parapets, all help to make a place from what
was just another dreary piece of the Regent's
Canal. It's all rather Robert Venturi of the late
1970s and is Farrell's most street-wise piece of
architecture. One can't imagine the building
anywhere else in London.

Place-making continues on the inside,
where inner spaces were treated as an open,
man-made landscape. Administration was on a
gallery floor and production facilities on the
ground. They shared an 'atrium-garden' whose
design theme progresses around the world, from
Japan to deserts – any place from which the
news comes. Its generous central stair, for
example, is in the form of a Mesopotamian
ziggurat. As a place for posing, and meeting it
became a set-piece regularly used for
programmes (thus bearing comparisons with
Imagination's much-used atrium). A cul-de-sac
at one end is a Dallas desert complete with
mirror glass facade; the hospitality lounge
evokes a Japanese temple; and so on.

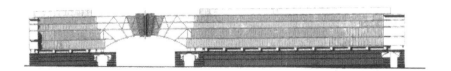

E20. Sainsbury supermarket and housing, 1988
17 Camden Road, NW1
Tube: Camden Town
Access: normal shop hours and private
Nicholas Grimshaw & Partners Ltd

There is a certain heroic quality about this supermarket complex striving to achieve a piece of urbane architecture appropriate to its context out of a brief better suited to some suburban fringe. It not only succeeds, but does so while offering its client a column-free trading hall and its customers ample underground car parking. The means employed are typical of Grimshaw: an acrobatic structure which becomes a principal feature of the architecture.

The articulation of the two storey bays to the main street frontage is intended to acknowledge the rhythm of the Georgian terrace opposite. Similarly, the canal to the rear of the site is provided with a sensitively scaled residential terrace made up of essentially conventional townhouses, although their aesthetic of curved aluminium and gasketed windows upsets some people. The inventiveness lies in the way a restrictive northern orientation has been addressed by means of incorporating roof lights and glazed, electrically operated garage doors to the double height living space. Just another piece of canal has become a place.

The western, service side of the complex is less successful, the relentless scale of the workshop strip overwhelming the smaller grain of existing street activities. Incidentally, it is on this side that one finds elaborate vehicle entry gates – competing, perhaps, with the post-modernism of Terry Farrell (Grimshaw's ex-partner) at TV-AM just along the street.

Apparently the client was less than impressed by the difficulties and costs of developing an inner city site – a comment on commercial criteria and an underscoring of the struggle undertaken by the architects. Perhaps this explains the battleship grey colouring, which – with a total avoidance of landscaping – lends an unnecessarily aggressive air to what is otherwise a thoughtful design.

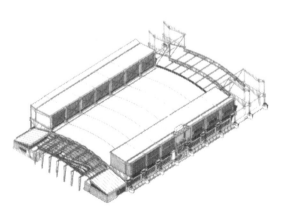

E21. Agar Studios, 1989
1 Cobham Mews, Agar Grove, NW1
Tube: Camden Town
Access: by appointment
David Chipperfield Architects

Chipperfield searches for fundamental, non-stylistic qualities in his work, arguing that a building 'should confirm values, not attempt to mystify. The basic elements have their own mystery'.

This development resulted from a classic piece of architectural opportunism recognising the potential of a former scrapyard off Agar Grove for the kind of small scale studios that proliferate in the Camden area (go around the corner, for example, to Camden Square, Camden Mews and Murray Mews, where one can find rows of architect's houses squeezed into rear garden plots). The site is triangular, enveloped by the rear gardens of the surrounding terraces.

The scheme comprises three parts: a pavilion; a central block of paired, two-storey units; and a long, low, single-storey block.

The two-storey studio units incorporate many of the basic features of Chipperfield's Japanese work, e.g. areas of render, exposed in-situ concrete and glass blocks set off against timber and simple steel detailing. Because of overlooking problems, the adopted strategy was to develop the site with large, loft-like spaces mainly lit from above. The entry facade has large areas of glass block punctuated by a horizontal run of clear glazing (reminiscent of the Maison de Verre, in Paris). In the centre are the wooden entry doors to the two main studio spaces, divided by a long concrete spine wall. These anchor the scheme and offer its principal focus upon arrival. The effect is at once both sparse and densely considered.

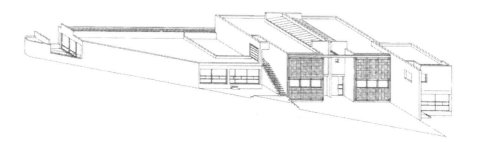

E22. Two houses by David Wild, 1984
44 Rochester Place, NW1
Tube: Camden Town
Access: private
David Wild

Home is where the heart is. And sometimes it
is a place to manifest one's aesthetic values and
architectural skills, too. David Wild did exactly
this in designing and building his own home in
Camden Town.

The house is comparatively small and
modest in character. But it carries within it an
intensity of expertise and artful consideration.
This could easily have produced an indigestibly
rich diet of frustrated ambition, but Wild has
meticulously sifted through his scheme with the
obsessiveness and tenacity one associates with
all extraordinary architecture. The result is a
residence which simultaneously excites,
architecturally, while producing a profound
sense of calm and well-being. Now this is
architecture!

A neighbour was impressed: could the
architect also do a house for him? So now there
are two similar houses side by side, each
terminating their half of the terrace and
separated by a tiny gap.

Their mentor is clearly Le Corbusier,
although the entry into a small, dark lobby
leading through to the better lit spaces above is
pure Frank Lloyd Wright. The spaces inside are
complexly interwoven, but clarity is never
sacrificed.

The outsides, although given great
consideration are simple rendered forms.
Wild's own house, No. 44, employs a cutaway
corner with a tall concrete column supporting
the upper studio floor – producing what Wild
terms a rotational asymmetry. The facade of
No. 42 is intended to create a balanced
composition sitting boldly at the end of Reed
Place.

These houses are the creation of an
architect who deserves more attention and more
commissions.

Four more in Camden

E23. Jazz Café, 1990
5 Parkway, NW1
Tube: Camden Town
Chassay Wright

E24. Bruges Place, 1988
Baynes Street, NW1
Tube: Camden Town
Jestico + Whiles

E25. Crowndale Centre, 1989
Mornington Crescent, NW1
Tube: Mornington Crescent
Rock Townsend

E26. One Off Studios, 1991
62 Chalk Farm Road, NW1
Tube: Chalk Farm
Ron Arad Associates

Camden Town is one of the liveliest areas of London, particularly at the weekend. These four projects are all part of the continual process of incremental redevelopment and refurbishment in the area.

E23. Jazz Café

Access: normal opening hours
The Jazz Café is incongruously housed within a former neo-classical bank building. The architects have appropriated its bourgeois pomposity and inserted into it an excellently designed set of places and spaces: a bar, restaurant gallery and stage set. Simple changes of level, floating ceilings, bright colours offset against natural materials and touches of neon provide the right touches to a robust environment.

Like all such places, one has to go there for the music and the people as well as the architecture – which otherwise always lies limply until the power comes on and the people arrive.

E24. Bruges Place

Access: private
This scheme is a fine example of inner city regeneration on a site that had been derelict for some thirty years. The scheme was entirely privately funded and strives to cope by means of sensitively mixing uses. The design integrates light industrial space with apartments and maisonettes above in two blocks of four storeys each, astride a central mews. Each of these blocks is a paired set of units around an access spine.

The geometrically organised fenestration and regular bands of contrasting blockwork suggest a rational, organised architectural scheme which clearly bears references to German housing of the early 1980s.

It is an urbane design, but schemes like this have to be incredibly robust and there is an acute disparity between the residential accommodation and what happens on the ground floor. Nevertheless it is a very welcome introduction of mixed uses on one site – something that would have been impossible without the particular expertise and negotiating skills of the designers.

E24

E23

E25. Crowndale Centre

Access: normal office hours

Crowndale was an appropriate commission for a practice known for its economic, enabling work with local authority projects. This project – designed by Charles Thompson, the partner in charge – is a conversion of a substantial but redundant Edwardian post-office building. Rock Townsend have carved out the interior and formed a new atrium from which an escalator leads up to the council offices. These are supplemented by an outer periphery of shops, cafes and some apartments, together with a health centre located in a smaller, separate building. The whole totals 11,000sq.m and accommodates 400 people.

The large curved roof (cantilevered from supports around the atrium's edge) and the add-on features signal the massive changes that have been wrought. It works well, but the scheme became caught up in struggles between central and local government and one detects the underlying dispiritedness of the long distance runner for whom things didn't quite go as planned.

E25

E26. One Off Studio

Access: by appointment

Ron Arad is an idiosyncratic, taciturn designer best know for radical exercises in chair design. His One Off Studio occupies an old building in a back-of-terrace mews just north of the Camden market area – an appropriate location for a conversion project that one might expect to find in Venice, LA, rather than Chalk Farm. It is an uncompromising building that a master like Bruce Goff would not have been ashamed of, although one suspects that Arad wonders what people are fussing about.

Finding the place and climbing its rusty access stair up to the first floor showroom and studio is like entering Dickensian London. Beyond the front door, however, is a world of steel joists with half severed, twirling ends; of a timber floor that waves like some ocean swell; and a studio space wrapped in a pre-fabricated tensile fabric and expanded metal roof. It's cheap, it's cheerful, it's exploratory, inventive and nutty. Thank God for that.

At weekends the vibrant Camden Market is just south of the One Off Studio.

E26

Around Hampstead Heath and beyond

Hampstead Heath divides this part of north London. Most of our selection is on the eastern side, extending north to Highgate. On the western, Hampstead Village, side are Mather's ZeNW3 and the Chassay/Wilson Blackburn house. The Burton house is near Kentish Town tube; Coutts Crescent and the Laurier road residence are not far from Parliament Hill. The Highgate group practice is near Highgate Village and Lubetkin's Highpoint blocks.

Out beyond means Walthamstow and, further to the most northern of our selections, at Epping, near the M25.

Suggested itinerary:
Highgate Group Practice (E33)
Coutts Crescent (E32)
Weinreb house (E30)
van Heyningen/Haward house (E28)
Burton house (E27)
Nightingale house (E31)
Blackburn house (E29)

Bisterne Avenue (E34)
Walthamstow Coroner's Court (E35)
Epping Town Hall (E36)

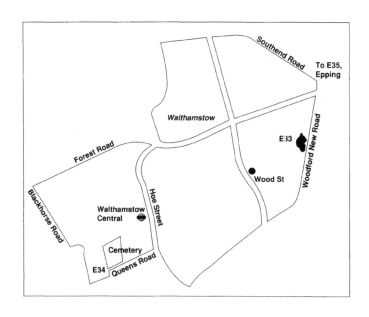

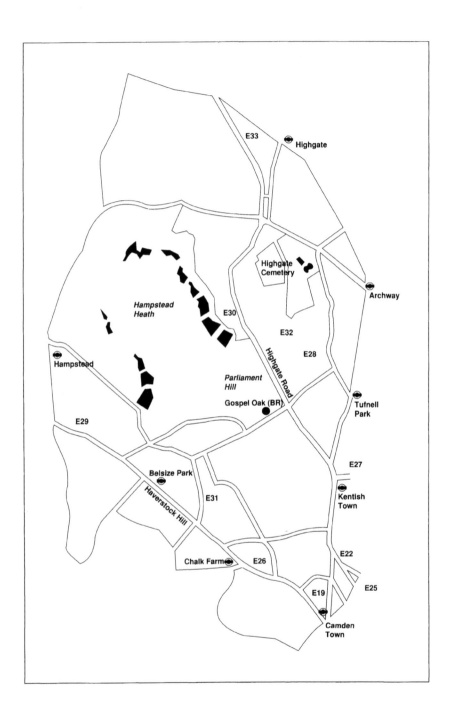

E33

Highgate

Highgate
Cemetery

Archway

Hampstead
Heath

E30

E32

E28

Hampstead

Parliament
Hill

Gospel Oak (BR)

Highgate Road

Tufnell
Park

E29

E27

Belsize Park

Kentish
Town

Haverstock Hill

E31

E22

Chalk Farm

E26

E25

E19

Camden
Town

Five private houses

E27. Burton house 1989
1b Lady Margaret Road, NW5
Tube: Kentish Town
Ahrends, Burton and Koralek

E28. van Heyningen/Haward house 1988
1c Laurier Road, NW5
Tube: Kentish Town
van Heyningen and Haward

E29. Blackburn house, 1988
Rosslyn Mews, NW3
Tube: Belsize Park
Peter Wilson and Tchaik Chassay

E30. Weinreb house 1989
16 Millfield Lane, N6
Tube: Kentish Town
CTS - Douglas Clelland & Gavin Rae

E31. Nightingale house 1988
30A Parkhill Road, NW3
Tube: Belsize Park
Hugh Cullum Richard Nightingale

The Camden Town/Kentish Town area appears to have more architects per square mile than anywhere else in London – many of them looking for opportunities to build for themselves.

One of the most notable houses in the area is that by John and Val Winter, a 1969 modernist exercise in glass and brown Cor-ten steel peeking over a high Victorian wall and overlooking Highgate Cemetery. Among those constructed more recently we have chosen four visible from the street which offer contrasting interpretations of site and configuration. Three are by architects for themselves, and one is by an architect and his photographer client for the latter's home and studio. Each demonstrates a concern with space and light as primary architectonic elements; but, beyond that, each is different.

Such houses are invariably only realised after substantial effort and opposition – they manifest much more than just design skill. Each can be seen from public highways and each has been regularly visited by Architectural Tours. If you go to look at them, please be discreet – these are homes, not public buildings.

E27. Burton house
Access: private

This house by Richard Burton for himself and his wife Mireille is a classic piece of urban infill and architectural opportunism: an end-of-terrace garden plot, south facing and with the potential only an architect keen to design for himself could envisage and realise.

Externally, the residence presents a high garden wall penetrated by a Chinese moon gate announcing the entrance. This leads to a small court dominated by a large tree; on one side is the garage with studio above; on the other is the kitchen /dining room of the main block. This external lobby area leads to a south-facing conservatory with sliding doors which runs the entire length of the house and gives access into the main living spaces.

The house is about as environmentally 'green' and energy efficient as one could get. Heavily insulated and constructed in timber, the conservatory buffers and tempers the environment marvellously. In somewhere like L.A. the house might be less remarkable. But it's not. It is in a north London Victorian suburb and all the more special because of it.

E27

E27

E28. van Heyningen/Haward house

Access: private

This is the second studio-house built by the
architects for themselves. The first (around the
corner in York Rise) insinuates itself between
two end of-terrace-gardens; the Laurier Road
house is sited at the end of a Victorian terrace
and has a more explicit urban role to fulfil.

The architects have continued the general
configuration of the terrace, but enter from the
gable end. The plan is a bi-axial set of rooms
straddling a stair and service core rising through
all floors. Children have the lower level
adjacent to the garden; the family kitchen and
the parent's bedroom/living room is on the next
level (a double height galleried space); at the
top is the studio – again a double height space,
complete with a mezzanine within the roof
pitch. It is all very compact, economically
arranged, and artfully handled.

E28

E29. Blackburn house

Access: private

The owners of this small building off
Hampstead High Street (David and Janice
Blackburn) would claim it is only meaningful as
an extension to their main residence around the
corner – the urban equivalent of a garden
pavilion or guest house where visitors are
entertained, parties held, art works enjoyed, and
study undertaken.

E29

The ground floor is used as an office.
The two upper floors – accessible by a staircase
which establishes a presence in the courtyard as
a large protruding bay window set at an acute
angle – are the reception suite/guest house. The
kitchen, dining area and living room are
arranged as one long space on the top floor.
The residual guest residence functions are
accommodated on the intermediate floor.

E29

The art intrudes everywhere, making
Blackburn House a small contemporary
equivalent of the whole series of such places
from Burlington's Chiswick Villa to Philip
Johnson's New Canaan house. The architecture
takes its place as an artful contribution,
although some of the detailing (e.g. around
radiators and staircases) was probably more
inspirational as a drawing than as a three-
dimensional construction.

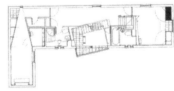

E29

E30. Weinreb house

Access: private

This house for a bachelor-photographer is squeezed between the 1950s home of Matthew Weinreb's parents (Ben Weinreb is author of the London encyclopaedia) and the site boundary.

The part of the house one sees from the gate is the front end of a tall, five-cube space that extends back into the site. Its upper storey is a front-to-back *piano nobile*, top-lit living space. The finish is untreated hardwood. On the roof is a terrace.

The interior is designed as a piece of habitable architectural joinery in MDF – all niches, drawers that are also hinged, cupboards that are also doors, secret panels, and peek-through openings to subsidiary spaces off the main one.

The place is testimony to what can be achieved when a skilled architect and an intelligent, collaborative client get together.

E30

E30

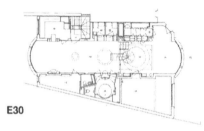

E30

E31. Nightingale house

Access: private

Like the Weinreb house, this residence for a bachelor architect is also on a small (4.5m) site. It squeezes itself in-between two other houses, one new, the other Georgian. A basic design limitation was to keep its height below that of the existing entry porch.

On the outside, a double height canted bay window provides scale to cope with the adjacent porch. The lower fenestration is banded, running through to a rusticated lower floor.

Internally, the design scheme centres around a double height living space topped by a skylight. On one side, toward the street, is the kitchen and dining area; on the other is the garden. Toward a flank wall is a stove, behind which a stair rises to an upper gallery area with study; the bathroom and bedroom are at the street end, above the kitchen.

E31

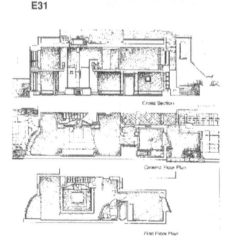

Cross Section

Ground Floor Plan

First Floor Plan

E31

E32. Coutts Crescent, 1989
13-23 St. Alban's Road, Highgate, NW5
Tube: Kentish Town
Access: private
Chassay Architects

This is a terrace of houses set in a street
characterised by inter-war semi-d's. While they
line the street with bland anonymity, Coutts
Crescent sets out to create a genuine sense of
urbane place and occasion.

The development is in the form of a three
storey crescent, arcaded at the lower levels. At
each end there is a tall studio house topped with
a curved roof accessible from a small loggia.
These 'bookends' each have a double height
bedroom/study overlooking the street from a
forecourt which separates the building from the
street (and facilitates car parking). It's all very
elegant and not what one expects midst
suburban semi's.

E32

E33. Highgate Group Practice, 1986
44 North Hill, Highgate, N6
Tube: Highgate
Access: by appointment
Douglas Stephens & Partners

There is a quality about this atrium group
practice suggesting it was drawn in an elegant,
thin freehand. Unlike Penoyre and Prasad's
backlands group practice, this is a detached
brick pavilion fronting the street. The facade is
simplicity itself: a simple brick gable over a
large glazed entry, leading through to an atrium
waiting area. The latter has been designed as an
outside space and all references to a medical
language were forbidden. Secondary facilities
are unobstrusively tucked away around the
perimeter of the principal spaces.

E33

*Lubetkin and Tecton's Highpoint
apartment blocks are nearby.*

*Café Mozart in Swain's Lane or Café
on Hampstead Heath is there for those in need
of a coffee.*

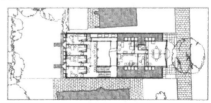

E33

E34. Bisterne Avenue apartments, 1991
Bisterne Avenue, E17
British Rail: Wood Street, Walthamstow
Access: private
Wickham Associates

The architect of this project, Julyan Wickham, is one of London's better architects who established himself designing bars and restaurants, and did not realise larger buildings until the advent of Horselydown in Butler's Wharf. About the same time, he obtained the commission to design this small block of six welfare flats near the Northeast London Polytechnic. The cross-references and common stylistic concerns show. If you like one building, then see the other.

The scheme provides decent accommodation of a type becoming increasingly rare in the UK. Walk-up stairs divide the building into two offset blocks of three flats each – one per floor. Living rooms and bedrooms get the ends and have balconies; kitchens and bathrooms act as intermediary buffers on either side of the access stair. The design is civilised, simple, and expertly considered. It strikes an urbane note in this area of suburban semi-ds.

But one can't please all the people all the time. Residents might like the accommodation, but the local authorities became very upset by the orange and blue rendered walls. Hopefully, the colours will still be the same when you visit.

E35. Walthamstow Coroner's Court, 1989
Queen's Road Cemetery, E17
Tube: Walthamstow Centre
Access: normal office hours/restricted
Tim Ronalds

This new coroner's court sits outside the gate to the Queen's Road Cemetery. It allows a reinterpretation and extension of an existing courthouse building, almost doubling the size of the facility. In particular, it provides a new hall to cope with up to 100 people who might visit the court, with an office area and associated storeroom, toilets, etc.

What makes this project special is Ronalds' manner of creating something worthwhile out of both a small programme and budget. There is a sense of occasion and calm, quiet dignity, of architecture doing its job without rhetoric and redundant gestures.

One enters into a small, paved external forecourt and is confronted by a square portico which has clearly learned from Asplund and Lewerentz's example at the Woodland Cemetery in Stockholm. But this is a fraction of the size. The aesthetic of simply articulated openings in large areas of plain brickwork similarly recalls Alvar Aalto. Fenestration is stained black, so that the hole in the wall quality is emphasised. One goes through the main door into a tall, holding lobby which is also square; off it are the office and service areas; a change of axis leads visitors through to the refurbished coroner's court.

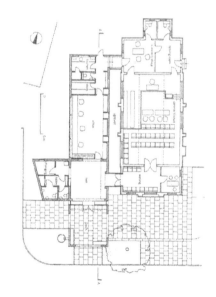

Other buildings to visit by Tim Ronalds include the Jacksons Lane Theatre, N6 (a conversion within a former church complex), and a small facility for disabled gardeners in Chomley Wood, N6. Both illustrate the same skill and expertise manifest on the Walthamstow Coroner's Court although, in the former case, there is more of Le Corbusier's influence at work, while the Chomley Wood building is a pitched roof timber structure which blends into the streetscape.

E36. Epping Town Hall, 1990
High Street, Epping
Tube: Epping
Access: normal office hours
Richard Reid Architects

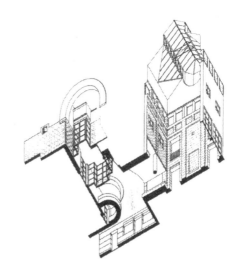

New town halls are rare projects in an era of centralising state government's erosion of local government authority. This one appears to owe something to the inspirations of architects such as Jim Stirling and, perhaps, Terry Farrell – one can imagine either of them tackling this complex of accommodation with a similar approach. In fact, it is designed by Richard Reid, a skilled architect who cross-fertilises vernacular sentiments and images with the ordering principles of high architecture. He was an appropriate selection for this small town in London's green-belt which represents much that is quintessentially English.

Apart from brightly coloured window frames, the Stirling influence is evident in the rationale for a brick tower dominating the building and the area – the signifier of an important local institution. It joins in an architectural dialogue with other historic towers further along the(former) village high street.

The tower is one of a number of elements intended to present themselves forward of a wall running through the complex, parallel to the street, i.e. they place themselves in the public realm while, behind the wall, are the offices of the bureaucracy. The former

elements include the main entry porch, the council chamber, staff recreation spaces, and an existing Victorian building, as well the tower. They are all rendered, but the background wall is in brick.

Ultimately, however, the finished building fails to realise the promise of its design scheme, betraying struggles against budgetary constraints, modern construction technologies and the erosive local politics common to this kind of commission (see the Crowndale Centre in Camden). But go and see it: there aren't many new buildings of this type or ambition in the UK.

F. Going west

Until the mid-nineteenth century most people in London lived within walking distance of the City. Then railways came to the centre's periphery and, not long after, underground routes under and across the city, and out to new suburbs. Together, these new forms of mass transport coped with an urban growth which more than tripled London's population between 1850 and 1911 (it had taken 150 years to achieve the previous tripling from the comparatively small figure of 600,000 which, in 1700, still made London the wonder of Europe).

The first underground lines (forming the Circle Line) looped the prosperous urban core which had been developed over the previous two hundred years or more. Much of the architecture of the 1980s described in previous sections has featured as part of the redevelopment of this inner area that would

have been familiar to architects such as Nash and Soane.

Much of the remainder lies in a widening band heading west on an axis between Westminster and Heathrow Airport – the current port of entry to London – through an area of Victorian suburbs and later inter-war sprawl which became known as Greater London. This area was contained by the creation of a 5-10 mile wide green belt wrapping the capital (and coinciding with the economic limitations of the underground). It divides London into an older, machine-age core and an extended, complex information-age metropolis which planners are still coming to terms with.

The buildings listed mainly break into two groups: those around Hammersmith; and those around Heathrow Airport.

Suggested itineraries:
Thames Wharf Studios (F1)
St Mary's Church, Barnes (F2)
The Ark (F3)
Metropolis Studios (F4)

Stockley Park (F5 - 11 inc.)
Bedfont Lakes (F12)
Richmond Riverside (F13)
Homebase (F15)
Sterling Hilton Hotel (F14)

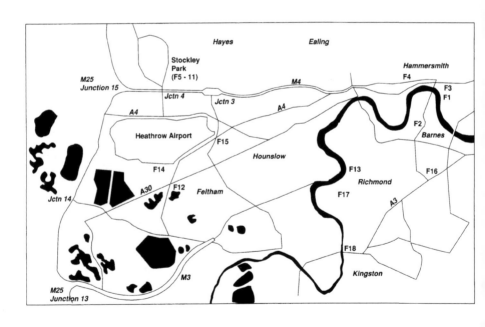

We have noted four recent buildings of particular interest in Hammersmith: Sir Richard Roger's warehouse-conversion studios and the related surrounding development (Thames Wharf Studios); Ted Cullinan's rebuilding and refurbishment work at St. Mary's Church, in Barnes; Julian Powell-Tuck's conversion work which created Metropolis Studios, off Chiswick High Street; and that outstanding landmark building, Ralph Erskine's Ark.

The latter is not only the one entirely new construction, but is also the most novel building.

One can walk between these buildings, but they are not adjacent and we advise using public transport.

The buildings around Heathrow are best accessed via car. Stockley Park, for example, is a motorway-accessible business park; Nicholas Grimshaw's Homebase building is an out-of-town shed; Bedfont Lakes is another business park intended to be served from the M25. The Sterling Hilton hotel can be accessed from the underground, although it too is meant for vehicular access.

Other buildings in west London include two houses which are also best seen by car and two town centre developments – the John Lewis store in Kingston and the Riverside development in Richmond – which are accessible by train and/or underground.

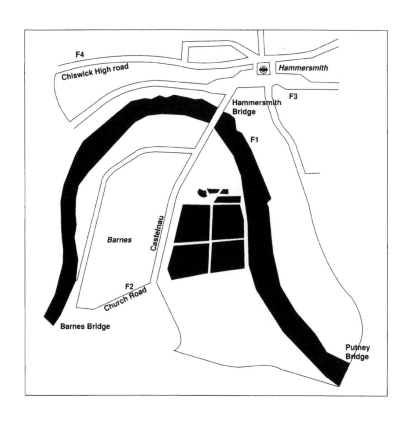

F1. Thames Wharf Studios, 1984
Thames Wharf, Rainville Road, W6
Tube: Hammersmith
Access: By appointment
Richard Rogers Partnership

The offices of Richard Rogers Partnership are part of a larger development (Thames Wharf Studios) taking in old riverside warehousing and new apartment blocks close to Hammersmith Bridge, on the north side of the river. The site was formerly an oil refinery.

The complex comprises older warehouses for studios and offices (Thames Wharf, managed by a Rogers subsidiary company); a new, single storey building to the east; a 1950s warehouse taken over by the practice and converted for their own offices; and three blocks of apartments. The River Café – run by Ruth Rogers and Rose Gray – acts as a social focus to the complex, attracting people from a wide area.

Juxtaposed on top of the practice offices squats a glazed and barrel-vaulted penthouse that reads like a truncated copy of the Lloyd's atrium. In the architects' words, 'Colours are used sparingly to highlight structure and service without detracting from the focus of the river.' In high summer, however, this vaulted structure is replete with large and very bright yellow sun-screening sails which some observers have considered rather obtrusive. But at least the practice's work is positive and optimistic, not reticent or tentative.

The three adjacent apartment blocks have two apartments per floor and are accessible by stair and lift cores on the street side. The river frontage is divided into a square grid and is largely glazed. Terraces are slung between the blocks (so as not to obscure the views). These blocks have a spartan air, the balconies, for example, suggesting a confrontational approach to lazing about by the river. But observe the top of the eastern-most block: here John Young – Rogers' partner – has his superlative penthouse, complete with a topmost circular bathroom walled in glass blocks.

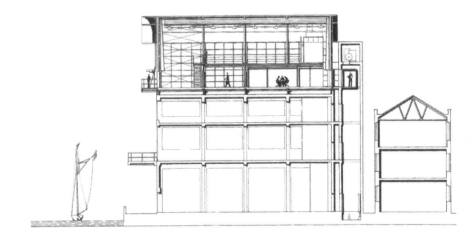

F2. St Mary's Church, Barnes, 1984
Church Road, SW13
British Rail: Barnes
Access: 10.30-12.30pm weekdays; 10.00-
12.00pm Sat & services Sun
Edward Cullinan Architects

Yesterday's news stales fast. Cullinan's work at St Mary's – now almost ten years old – gets somewhat neglected. Perhaps this is because it is both a religious building and one with evident Arts and Crafts overtones rather than commitments to hi-tech (not, one hastens to add, to be compared with Branson Coates' '21st century Arts and Crafts'). In fact, it is one of the Cullinan practice's better pieces of work.

The project involved an almost complete rebuilding of the church after its destruction by arson in 1978. Little was left after the fire except the tower and some outer walls, so that the Cullinan scheme is an entire rewriting of the church's architecture. Designs retaining the best of the historic fabric were evolved in close collaboration with the local community. The objective was to produce a space for congregation and worship that would continue the tradition established on the site in the 11th century, but 'without pastiche'.

Externally, the aesthetic is entirely English: reassuringly ecclesiastic, with large, steeply pitched slate roofs. It seems entirely in keeping with a part of Barnes that seems almost rural, although it is just across the river from buildings like the Rogers' office and the Ark at Hammersmith. Inside, its open spaces and complex roof timbers remind one of a post-modernist Charles Moore church in Los Angeles (similarly a replacement of one which burnt down). It's a wonderfully rich and substantial building – Cullinan at his best and, perhaps, his most comfortable.

The church gutted by fire

The church rebuilt

F3. The Ark, 1992
Talgarth Road, Hammersmith, W14
Tube: Hammersmith
Access: private
Ralph Erskine
Executive architects: Lennart Bergstrom
(Sweden) and Rock Townsend (UK)

The narrow erudition of mandarins, the sales
expertise of agents, and the logic of accountants
have cross-fertilised to emasculate and
institutionalise our ideas about the office as
workplace. In such a world, the Ark comes as
a small blessing.

London's new office buildings – whether
packaged in hi-tech or post-modern garb –
almost invariably derive from American models
and the realities of air conditioning, suspended
ceilings, access floors and a 1.5 m planning grid
arithmetically deployed across rectangular
chunks of deep space. The Ark, however, is a
Scandinavian implant and brings with it
different values. This is the elder Ralph
Erskine, sceptical of an instrumental logic
which quantifies and commodities everything,
lobbying for a more humane architecture.

The building is called the Ark because that
is what it looks like – some primeval, dark
brown vessel run aground, against a motorway
heading west to Heathrow. (The cladding is
actually copper and will eventually go green).
The pop-up tower above the roof, looking like a
submarine periscope, is a viewing platform.

Internally, the Ark has been conceived as an
open, multi-layered village of complex and
dramatic spaces – all Swedish blonde wood and
white surfaces – organised around a spectacular
atrium. The roof is not glazed, but floats across
the building's mass at an angle and sets up
clerestorey windows and terracing.

Throughout, Erskine offsets quality of place
against refinement of detailing. But one also
has to appreciate the Swedish origins which
lend Erskine's architecture open-ended,
pragmatic and almost opportunist qualities
deriving from struggles against controlling
industry influences – the architecture has to be
robust to erosion during the process of
development and construction, as well as in use.

F4. Metropolis Studios, 1990
9 The Powerhouse, 70 Chiswick High Rd, W4
Tube: Stamford Brook
Access: private
Powell Tuck, Connor & Orefelt Ltd

Metropolis is a most unusual recording studio. The enthusiasm it evokes and the satisfaction it provides are evident in the comments of recording engineers, who love the place.

This private studio occupies one part of a 1901 transport power station now converted to a multiplicity of uses. Visitors are received in a tall, side-lit atrium space providing access to all four floors and their five studios. Galleries, flying stairs, ramps and lift cages dominate one's impression. It all appears rather *ad hoc*: a mix of structural steel, steel decking, plywood and render. The aesthetic, however, originates in studio spaces where obtuse angles refract sound, and slices of acoustic absorbent line walls and fly about overhead. What appears arbitrary is, in essence, highly engineered.

The designer's job has been to organise and order, to formulate an appropriate, controllable language which can be adapted and tuned, even as it stimulates architectural pleasure.

The overall architectural configuration – a *parti* dominated by a differentiation between the tall atrium and the adjacent wall of studios – goes hand in hand with an articulative language dependent upon a selection of simple materials and expertise in construction. The atrium is mostly concrete and metal, a rather cold space which contrasts with the warmth of the render, timber and linen used in the studios.

The users are international recording engineers and artists who demand studios that can be pleasurably inhabited for long periods of time. It is rare that studios provide such a quality, but that is exactly what Metropolis offers them. It offers spaces and places that are a joy to work in, even contriving to get daylight into the studios. It is textural (compare the lift installation with the usual glitzy glass contraptions), robust, probably forgiving and certainly distinctive, but none of it gets in the way. Few London projects are a better justification of good design.

Stockley Park, Heathrow

F5. Buildings A1.1, A1.2, A2.1 and A2.3,
1986–89
Hillingdon, Middlesex
BR: West Drayton
Arup Associates

F6. Buildings A3.1, A1.3, A2.2, A3.2, B1, B5, B7, 1987–89
Hillingdon, Middlesex
BR: West Drayton
Arup Associates

F7. The Arena, 1989
Hillingdon, Middlesex
BR: West Drayton
Arup Associates

F8. Building B3, 1988
Hillingdon, Middlesex
BR: West Drayton
Sir Norman Foster & Partners

F9. Building B8, 1990
Hillingdon, Middlesex
BR: West Drayton
Ian Ritchie Associates

F10. Buildings B2/B4, 1991
Hillingdon, Middlesex
BR: West Drayton
Troughton MacAslan

F11. Building W3, 1991
Hillingdon, Middlesex
BR: West Drayton
Eric Parry Associates

Stockley is a typical dream park for business: an extravagantly planted landscape adjacent to a golf course, near to the M4 and the M25, and adjacent to Heathrow Airport. Only about 25% of the site is built upon – the rest is grass, lakes, sculpture, access roads and car-parking. And lots of security measures.

What one sees now is a latter-day equivalent to Nash's vision for Regent's Park, except that it is for business. The park is populated by isolated buildings of varying size, all conforming to an underlying typology researched and formulated originally by DEGW, who were responsible for the original master plan concept before Arup's took over.

But not so long ago the place was an unsightly, polluted waste dump created from infill to former gravel pits. That was before information technology and Silicon Valley, before the vision of Stuart Lipton, the man most responsible for Stockley.

The first buildings were by Arup Associates; later came the Arena community building, also by Arups. Other buildings – by a host of significant British practices – have mostly adopted a more strident note. The SOM contribution is mostly on the westernmost part of the site. Ove Arup were the civil engineers; landscaping was by Bernard Ede and Charles Funke.

Each of the buildings manifests a struggle between the developer's equation and an attempt to offer something with idiosyncratic character – the percentage for architecture. They make quite a showcase.

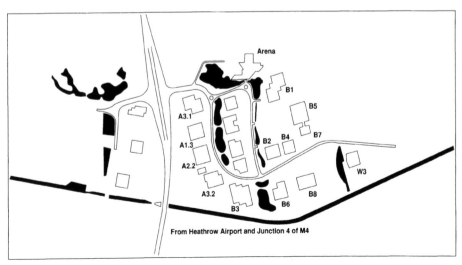

F5. Buildings A1.1 , A1.2, A2.1 and A2.3
Access: private

These are the first range of buildings in
Stockley. They represent the original concept
of what the park's buildings would be like and
possess a balance of expert design, good
landscaping and economy which generates a
note at odds with the later buildings. The
smallest (A1.1) is 37,000 sq. ft; the largest
(A2.1) is 51,000. In these earlier buildings, the
user-research carried out by DEGW was a
fundamental informant of the architecture. It
later became somewhat diluted, when
'signature' architects took over.

F6. Buildings A3.1 , A1.3, A2.2, A3.2, B1, B5, B7.
Access: private

These later Arup buildings are no longer
adjacent to the lakes. All are to the west of the
lakes and the access road to this part of the
park. All are larger than the first buildings: the
smallest (A1.3) is 50,000 sq. ft; the largest
(A2.2) is 114,000. It has been commented that
they manifest a new note – less attractive,
larger, more dense, less pleasant in terms of a
relationship of building to parkland, more
confused access arrangements, more brutal
relationship of parking to building.

F7. The Arena
Access: private

This is the'community building with
management offices, sports club, shops and

F5

restaurants – the social focus of Stockley,
located where Park and golf course come
together. The *parti* is an arrangement of
accommodation centred upon a rotunda.
Curiously, its paradigm is the medieval castle.
Pedestrians approach the rotunda's brick walls
by crossing over a drawbridge and moat; one
then enters an arcade, above which is a top-lit
gallery. On the opposite side, the citadel's walls
are broken down, so that the building opens up
to car parking(the wheeled approach). It is an
excellent building which suffers from the
contradiction between its community function
and the social realities of Stockley.

F7

F8. Building B3

Access: private

This building is one of Stockley's larger buildings and has, as one might expect, a simple and effective *parti*. Three blocks of 18m wide accommodation (totalling 120,000sq. ft) run in parallel; two atria lie in-between; services are located at the rear (southern) end of each office block. The structural concept employs centrally place Y shaped elements, each of which is 27m across. Roof lights are at the high points (over the atria), and gutters at the low.

F8

The totally glazed, silicone-jointed cladding attempts to reinforce a perimeter circulation route keeping desks (and junk) away from the perimeter. Unfortunately, this hardly supports efficient space planning and the inevitable has happened: the tenants' desks are now against the glazing. It uses fritting of ceramic discing to cope with solar gain. The idea is a transfer from auto technology and is equally unsuccessful on a building.

F9. Building B8

Access: private

This is a simple three-storey air-conditioned building with a rectangular plan and a central atrium. At either end are steel-clad service cores, but the remainder of the building is entirely glazed. This glazing is also fritted in order to mask visual clutter in the spandrel zone.

F9

The 9m-square structural bay is boldly extended in order to support large, perforated stainless steel sunscreening louvres on three sides. This might be the percentage for architecture, but it gives an effective image.

F10. Buildings B2 / B4:

Access: private

The major architectural effect of this building is created by its solar-shading sails. These hang upon an elegantly proportioned three-storey facade, the lower storey of which sits on piloti (as the Parry building). External escape stairs help to provide further articulation.

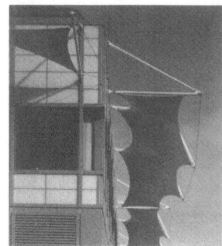

F10

F11. Building W3

Access: private

All the Stockley buildings with sub-tenancies effectively take the landlord's pervasive control through into the entrance lobbies and up to the individual tenant's doors. The building architect can design the shell and this lobby, but has to leave the tenancy spaces for separate fit-out. In Parry's building, this offered the opportunity to provide the best lobby in the park – a place where the designer's struggle against the developer's equation at last wins more than a few Brownie points.

Simply skewing the geometry of the building's two rectangular blocks of office accommodation provided sufficient to work with. This device provides the intermediary spatial material which Parry's practice works with. But it is the detailed consideration – the layering and selection of materials – which then provides the quality of excellence.

Externally, the building is raised up on piloti, then infilled with clear glazing. The modernist note continues in the character of the cladding to the upper levels, where a mix of clear glass and glass block extends a recurring theme in contemporary British architecture derived from the Maison de Verre.

Other buildings in business park are B6 by Geoffrey Darke Architects, B7 by Peter Foggo Associates and SOM's Glaxo buildings in Stockley Park West.

F12. Bedfont Lakes, 1992
Bedfont Lakes, Staines, Middlesex
Tube: Heathrow Terminal 4, BR: Feltham
Access: private
Edward Cullinan Architects
Michael Hopkins & Partners

Bedfont Lakes is southeast of Heathrow Airport
and not far from the M25. Like Stockley Park,
to the north, it exploits these locational
opportunities.

Hopkins' masterplan is simple: two U-
shaped blocks divided into three units, modelled
on the traditional urbane London square rather
than the usual Silicone Valley precedent of
buildings in a parkland. The blocks are
arranged around a central landscaped parking
area utilising the hollow of a former gravel pit
to create a double height car park.

One half of the development called New
Square is by the Ted Cullinan practice; the
other (occupied by IBM, shown middle right) is
by Michael Hopkins' practice. The buildings
couldn't be more different.

Cullinan's architecture is constrained into a
Beaux-Arts strait-jacket of symmetry and a play
with central entry features and picturesque corner.
It is well designed, but his three buildings are
overshadowed by Hopkins' buildings.

The three IBM units are an impressive
exercise in a cool, blue-black aesthetic of steel
and glass. A steel-and-glass architect like Craig
Ellwood would have immensely enjoyed it.
This is a thick hi-tech – a kind of architecture
that exhilarates and lifts the spirit. The
carefully considered detailing is superb. This is
the real thing.

One building dominates : a central block
within which is a galleried atrium with an
Aalto-like stair and a set of lifts and glass-block
lobby floors similar to what was provided by
Hopkins at Bracken House. The slung glazed
roof (the structure is on the outside) is solar-
protected by fabric sails. To one side of the
atrium space is a cafeteria; the other is for
marketing and exhibitions.

The side blocks act as independent and
separate wings. All three buildings employ a
space-packing strategy which plans three people
to a desk and depends entirely upon
sophisticated information technologies.

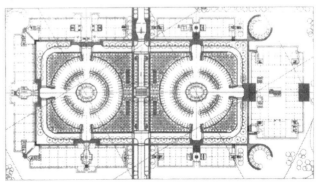

F13. Richmond Riverside, 1987
Riverside, Heron Square, Richmond, Surrey
Tube: Richmond
Access: courtyards only
Erith and Terry

Quinlan Terry's picturesque exercise in neo-Palladianism has been castigated because, in reality, its outer forms conceal bog-standard contemporary offices. Perhaps this is unfair. Complexes such as Broadgate and Canary are not very different packaging exercises around a common equation. And is Terry's ambition so different from the retention of facades, behind which lies a new piece of architecture?

The problem is the manner of packaging. Terry's apparent architectural offence is to attempt the disguise of a large block of contemporary offices and shops as an aggregation of authentic Georgian buildings – to produce an historical sham. Rock Townsend attempted something similar at the Angel, where a large beast is fractured into a multiplicity of post-modern facades; no one complains of that ambition, only of the lack of success. Terry might argue that he is merely designing in his preferred idiom and attempting no deceit.

Perhaps the real complaint is that he is failing to renew the struggle to realise a thoroughly contemporary language, hiding instead in some dim, past ambience of reassurance. But surely it is impossible for him to be anything other than contemporary – in situation, constructional techniques, project management, clientele, and the rest. Why not congratulate Terry for ameliorating the offensive two-dimensional quality of developer's briefs, for offering the pretence of a more fragmentary, incremental, accessible and humanly scaled architecture. Because it is a lie? Then what of the validity of the offices behind? Are we meant to celebrate these ubiquitous, hardly habitable spaces lying sandwiched between suspended ceilings and raised access floors? Are they not a lie of another kind?

Such are the issues in determining authenticity. Perhaps Terry should, at least, be allowed credit for artfulness and expertise. And it certainly takes courage to go against the political grain. Shame, though, about the lack of true organicity in the scheme.

F14. Sterling Hilton Hotel, 1990
Terminal Four, Heathrow Airport
Tube: Terminal 4 Heathrow
Access: public
Manser Associates

This was originally built as the Sterling (you
can still see the holes in the cladding where the
sign was). You'd be forgiven for thinking it
was also first built as Foster's Sainsbury Centre
near Norwich.

It was Goodhart-Rendel who remarked
that it is important to differentiate between
imitation (betraying a lack of originality) and
the transmutation of influences (manifesting
originality). He also noted that the original
might be otherwise unsuccessful; and that the
unoriginal can be highly valuable and
satisfactory. Perhaps the Hilton comes into the
latter category, but it is a sufficiently inventive
transmutation to be argued into the former.

Foster's original is an open-ended
structural tube; the heart is a great hall and the
long sides accommodate secondary facilities
(the servant spaces); each gable is a wall of
glass. Mansell's practice has adapted and
reinterpreted his *parti* by placing the 397 hotel
bedrooms in the sides and employing the space
in the centre as a five-storey, 30m wide atrium
accommodating public facilities: reception,
restaurants and bar (another paradigm involved
here is the American Hyatt series of hotels
designed by John Portman); half the bedrooms
face out, and half face into the atrium. The plant
is housed in a basement.

Cleverly, the scheme lessens the bulk of
the gables of the wings by sliding the plan into
a trapezoid. This facilitates a handling of the
end elevation which begins to approach the
slender proportions achieved by Foster.
Another difference is the cladding. Whereas
Foster uses a sophisticated and expensive
cladding system, the Mansell practice employs
a low-cost metal stud framed construction faced
with a rain-screen of self-finished cement
particle boards.

The interiors are by Peter Glynn Smith
Associates.

F15. Homebase, 1987
Syon Lane, Brentford, Middlesex
Tube: Boston Manor
Access: extended shopping hours
Nicholas Grimshaw & Partners Ltd

Whether Homebase is original or not seems besides the point (see F14). Its main significance is as an impressive piece of roadside architecture by the architect who was later to design British pavilion at Seville Expo and the Channel connection installation at Waterloo.

But you might ask whether this is what Venturi termed a duck or a decorated shed. In one sense it is the former – what you see is what you get: a large shed selling DIY goods. On the other hand, the structural acrobatics which distinguish the building and turn it into a big sign suggest it is a decorated shed.

Beyond such debates is an intriguing piece of hi-tech architecture enclosing some 4,200sq. m under a massive, column-free structure. This has three principal components: a 33m high mast flagging the tenant's name; a 75m span longitudinal spine beam which the mast supports; and a transverse structure of 11m wings brought down at the perimeter onto triangulated supporting structures. Over the spine beam runs a long roof light which drops down each side to produce what the designers term a slice of light.

It's an amazing piece of *bravura* whose antecedents include Rogers' Inmos factory in Wales. However, Grimshaw's building has been received as somewhat vulgar. Perhaps it is simply the associations with the tenant who, instead of producing expensive hi-tech chips by means of a leading-edge technology, sells cheap hi-tech tools and materials to a mass market.

F16. Fowler/Jestico house, 1988
5, Garden Close, Portsmouth Road, SW15
Tube: East Putney
Accessibility: private (by arrangement)
Vivien Fowler & Tom Jestico

This is a single storey house in the tradition of
open-plan, steel framed residences first seen in
California toward the end of WWII – a
favourite of architects when designing for
themselves. A key agenda they embrace is to
open the relationship between interior and
exterior. There are a few examples in London,
including John Winter's house outside the gates
of Highgate Cemetery; Georgie Wolton's and
Robin Spence's houses in Belsize Park; and
Michael Hopkins' home in Hampstead. Jestico,
too, has adopted this approach to house building
and its implicitly spacious way of living.

    This is a family house for the architect,
his wife (also a designer) and their teenage
family. It had to be robust.

    The building is effectively self-build –
without any main contractor and utilising high
quality, modern materials. It is also highly
energy-efficient, despite all the glazing.

F16

F17. Knight house, 1987
Arlington Road, Richmond, Surrey
Tube: Richmond
Access: private
David Chipperfield Architects

Nightmare on Arlington Road – the monster
they couldn't stop! A quiet, respectable post-
war detached home transmuted by its
photographer heir and his errant architect into a
local *cause célèbre*. The beast in question is a
masterfully crafted exercise in the sparse,
minimal aesthetics for which Chipperfield has
become so noted, resulting in the former
vernacular brick house metamorphosing into
something modernist, graceful and assertive.

F17

108

F18. John Lewis department store, 1990
Horse Fair, Kingston upon Thames, Surrey
British Rail: Kingston
Access: normal shop hours
Ahrends Burton and Koralek

Modern department stores are usually in new town or out of town shopping centre locations. This John Lewis site in Kingston is a mix of both: the place is an established suburban centre; and its core is undergoing radical transformation and 'modernisation'.

ABK's riverside scheme conceives of this large, 63,000sq. m store as a brick-walled edifice with massive amounts of internal daylighting. The large, open interior is arranged as a set of terraces linked by escalators – a merchandise showcase enhanced by the natural light. Daylight is even brought through to the lowest level supermarket, although the two stores are otherwise kept separate.

The *parti* of the scheme takes two large squares, sets their diagonally raking roofs back to back, and accommodates administration, service areas, lifts, escape stairs, air conditioning vent towers, etc. around the perimeter. Car parking is at basement level. A ring road around Kingston's centre, bisects the building at ground level. Here, on the exterior, ABK have had quite a challenge in articulating large areas of brickwork. The comparison to their achievement is the competitor, Bentalls, across the road – an exercise in post-modernist packaging.

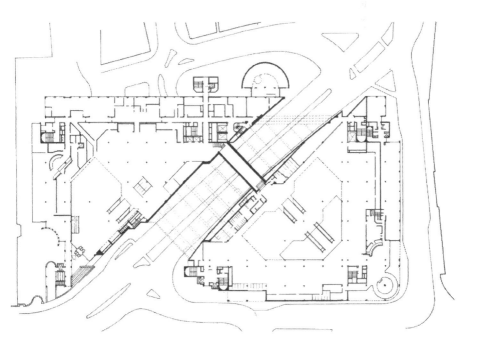

G. South of the Thames

Imperial War Museum (G1)
Lambeth Community Centre (G2)
Foster Offices (G3)
Bricklayer's Arms (G4)
Doctor's Surgery (G5)
Vining Street housing (G6)
Strathleven Street housing (G7)
Theatre, Carshalton (G8)

Covers a large area! Surprisingly, there is a comparatively low density of good contemporary architecture to see. However, this does not mean that you should ignore it.

The theatre buildings designed by Ted Cullinan's office are quite far south, but worth the effort. His Lambeth Community Care Centre is one of two similar small medical facilities, the other being the Whittington Day Care Centre in Polworth Road, SW16, near Streatham Common (not included, but also worth a visit).

The War Museum is also near to the Lambeth centre, just south of Waterloo Staion, where Nicholas Grimshaw's new terminal for the Channel Tunnel (H1) can be visited.

The East Croydon Station by Alan Brookes Associates (H3, see next section) is also quite far south. It is not far to the west of Cullinan's Carshalton Theatre. It is Redhill Station, however, that is our furthest south selection – it is equivalent to going north, to Epping Town Hall.

MacCormac Jamieson and Prichard's two housing schemes in Brixton are easily accessible.

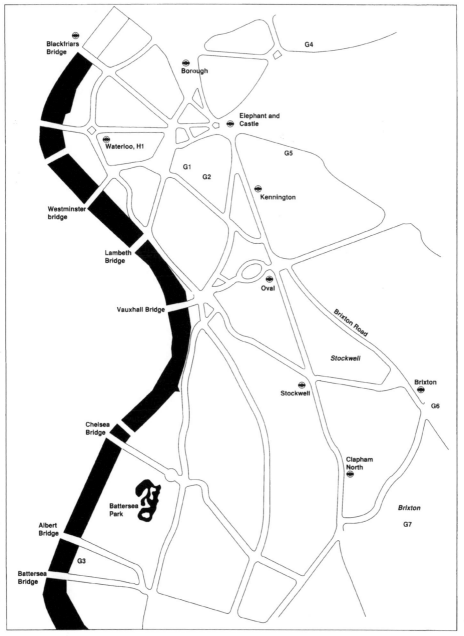

Blackfriars
Bridge

Borough

G4

Elephant and
Castle

Waterloo, H1

G5

G1

G2

Kennington

Westminster
bridge

Lambeth
Bridge

Vauxhall Bridge

Oval

Brixton Road

Stockwell

Brixton

Stockwell

G6

Chelsea
Bridge

Clapham
North

Battersea
Park

Brixton

Albert
Bridge

G7

G3

Battersea
Bridge

G1. Imperial War Museum, 1989
Lambeth Road, SE1
Tube: Lambeth North/Waterloo
Access: normal museum hours
Arup Associates

Practically everything Arup Associates does is worthy of attention. They are a large practice with outstanding skill. This conversion and refurbishment project for the Imperial War Museum (in what was once, ironically, the Bedlam Hospital for the insane, designed in 1812) is typical of Arups' work.

The key feature of this scheme is the creation of an excellent glazed atrium from a former light well in the heart of the building. Here are hung the aircraft and rockets of generations of modern warfare; below them are tanks, guns and the similar technology of warfare. The exposed brickwork of the surrounding accommodation has been cleaned up and these spaces are now effectively galleries to the atrium.

It has been argued that there is something implicitly obscene about war museums: they pander to pornographic appetites whilst ostensibly acknowledging and celebrating heroic wartime efforts. However, Arups handle it all in a most expert way. Nonetheless, perhaps their scheme lacks a certain bravura appropriate to coping with fast, dynamic and violent machines emasculated into some unmenacing cadaveric state. One can't help but compare the Museum with Frank Gehry's Aerospace Museum in LA, where airplanes are also hung – including on the facade. Imagine if Arups had dared to sling a plane on Sidney Smirke's Greek portico!

That said, this museum is excellent. Arups' roof over the former light well is typical of their structural masterfulness. Apart from the architecture, however, visit the museum for its art collection – that is unmissable.

The museum shop is by the practice of Ken Armstrong.

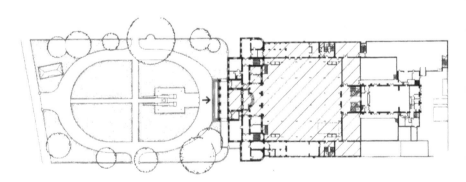

GROUND FLOOR
IMPERIAL WAR MUSEUM

G2. Lambeth Community Care Centre, 1985
Monkton Street, SE11
Tube: Lambeth North/Waterloo
Access: private; by arrangement
Edward Cullinan Architects

This community care facility – accommodating
a 20 bed community care centre, with day care
for 35 and its own therapy and nursing staff –
provides local hospital attention and specialist
medical services. It is an unusual commission
for the 1980s and has probably attracted more
attention from northern European architects
than British ones. But it is an especially
refreshing building, arising from a brief which
one suspects is far more appropriate to the skills
and appetites of the Cullinan practice than
office buildings such as that designed for
Bedfont Lakes.

The overriding impression is of an
architecture with meaning for its users. A lot of
dialogue has gone into the design; and the
architecture allows this dialogue to continue. It
is funky and homely; robust and forgivable.
People can possess it, work with it, and
properly inhabit it. The planning offers the
users a sense of place as well as practical
facilities and aesthetic considerations. There
has been no contradiction between serving the
users and providing good design. (If only more
architecture had these qualities).

On the lower floor are administrative and
consulting rooms; on the upper floor are suites
of small hospital rooms opening onto a south
facing terrace. Beyond that (unexpectedly for
this part of London) is a a large garden to which
Cullinan's design sets up a strong relationship.
In the centre of the building is a conservatory,
complete with over-stuffed second-hand
furniture. Some designers might find the
internal detailing less than refined or elegant
(and the furnishing policy of charity shop chic
somewhat tiresome); others will delight in it.
For us, it sets a bench-mark in true authenticity.

The outside can be readily seen, but
internal visits should be arranged through the
centre administrator. Please don't intrude.

*Also see Cullinan's similarly scaled
Whittington Centre in Polworth Road, Streatham.*

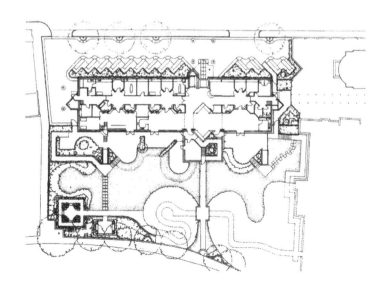

G3. Foster offices, 1990
Riverside Three, 22 Hester Road, SW11
Tube: Fulham Broadway
Access: by appointment
Sir Norman Foster and Partners

Located between the dreariness of Battersea Bridge and the frivolity of the Albert is the studio of the country's foremost hi-tech architect. It should be something special. On the inside it is; on the outside it is rather ordinary, so attempt to see the entrance stair and lobby, at least.

The eight-storey building stacks rentable office space off a public terrace, a splendid double height studio space, 30 apartments, and two penthouse/studios. The building is meant to be simple and elegant; but it appears rather mean, failing to evoke more interest than that this is the work of a famous architect. It is hardly a paradigm of mixed-use, living/working arrangements.

The studio interior, however, is a different story. The entry lobby is wide and Alvar Aalto-like. It accommodates a grand, long stair of four flights leading to a hangar-like studio space, entirely glazed and enjoying panoramic views over the river. Parallel to the stair is a long diner-bar at the top level (food and drink aren't allowed at the workplace); this overlooks occupants making their promenade up or down the stair.

The studio space is 60m long, 24 wide and 6.5 high. It is (not unexpectedly) refreshingly

rational, straightforward and, especially, humane. Here sit the workers at thirteen benches, each 11m long and set at right angles to the north facing wall of glass which offers panoramic views onto the river. Marching through the centre is a row of tall concrete columns. It's a memorable space which has been argued to have Wright's Johnson Wax interior as its reference.

Model-making, audio visual and presentation spaces, computer rooms and the like are all housed to the rear of the studio space. Filing and meetings are kept to a mezzanine above.

Around the corner at 53 Battersea Church Road is an interesting small house by Julian Powell-Tuck.

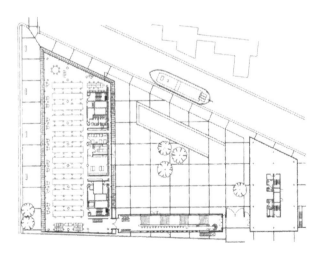

G4. Bricklayer's Arms, 1990
Mandela Way, SE1
Tube: Elephant & Castle
Access: private
David Richmond & Partners

This scheme ranks as one of the better examples
of industrial/warehousing development in
London – an artful example of image-conscious
developer architecture.

The scheme comprises a long range of
warehouse units neatly sliced into two
development phases by a diminutive public
cycle track. Both halves are similar, but phase
one places its truck access and employee
parking to the rear, whilst phase two reverses
this, providing them as a forecourt separated
from the street by a run of steel security fencing
(high security is one of the sales features).

Each range of buildings is broken into
separate units with identifiable front doors and
reception areas arranged around small
landscaped entry courts.

But what lift the entire scheme are two
significant architectural features. The first is
the treatment of the brick facades as a single run
– fractured where the entry courts are located as
glazed set-backs, and punctuated in such a way
that it reads as an infilled arcade. The second is
related: a run of steel beam section which
straddles the parapet and relentlessly winds its
way along the entire building, leaping across
the wide access court recesses and tying the
disparate tenancies into a cohesive unity. It is a
simple gesture: economic and effective; self-
evidently redundant and rhetorical; a
metaphorical string tying the architectural
parcel together and a literal example of added
value by design.

The cornice is terminated with rather art
deco-like features which add a more whimsical
note. But perhaps this is to carp about an
excellently designed and high quality scheme.

G5. Doctor's surgery, 1992
1 Manor Place, SE17
Tube: Kennington
Access: by appointment
Penoyre and Prasad

Any resemblance between the qualities of this incredibly dense, complex and tightly packed piece of architecture and Cullinan's Lambeth centre is more than coincidental – Penoyre and Prasad worked on that project too.

Manor Place also bears similarities with Patel and Taylor's Lauriston studios: both projects reveal little to the street and hide themselves away behind terracing; both demonstrate a similar tenacity, inventiveness and consideration.

The surgery hides behind a terraced corner junction and knits together two separate properties and a new backlands building into an organic whole. One enters from Manor Place, going through to the new, two storey building within what was once a builder's yard. Ahead, is a tight, double height reception area; behind and above this are the doctor's consultation rooms. Two overhead bridges provide links between the old and new facilities.

Since the site is hemmed in, getting daylight into rooms and corridors has been a difficult challenge successfully dealt with by clerestory windows, setbacks and glass floor blocks.

This is not a refined pursuit of technical brilliance, nor a demonstration of sophisticated constructional technique. All materials and finishes are simple – veritably cheap and cheerful. This is architecture resulting from a long dialogue with users, employing a vernacular construction mixed with much design ambition and perseverance. The occupants enjoy it because it considers them, caters for them, flatters them and uplifts them. Their needs and the architect's design ambition have not been in conflict.

If you go, be considerate and discreet – this is a working care centre. The practice has a similar project in Rayleigh Gardens SW2.

Two Housing projects in Brixton

G6. Vining Street housing, 1989
Vining Street, SW9
Tube: Brixton
MacCormac Jamieson Prichard

**G7. Strathleven & Mauleverer Road
housing** 1991
Strathleven Road, SW9
Tube: Brixton
MacCormac Jamieson Prichard

*These are two housing association schemes by
the practice of MacCormac Jamieson and
Prichard. The first – Vining Street – is to the
east of Lambeth Town Hall, in a dense urban
site; the other is just west, in possibly more
salubrious suburban Victorian streets. They
bear witness to the skill of the architects and
are good examples of considered urban infill
which integrates and repairs the existing fabric.*

G6. Vining Street housing, 1989
Access: private
The Vining Street scheme involved a difficult
brief for the site: a call from the community for
small houses with individual front doors, on a
familiar street pattern. The designers have
provided four types of maisonettes and
apartments (comprising 74 dwellings, all
carefully and independently articulated). While
this scheme could hardly be termed
contexturalist in the structuralist sense aspired
to by Fenella and Jeremy Dixon, there are
similarities with the terraced London house
types built by the Victorians (see St Mark's
Road).

G7. Strathleven & Mauleverer Road
Access: private
The scheme at Strathleven and Mauleverer
Streets (they form adjacent blocks along
existing streets) provides 42 dwellings of ten
variable types (including for the elderly and
disabled). The scheme is informed by similar
concerns and values to those dealt with at
Vining Street.

G7

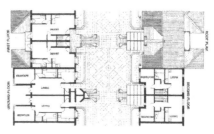

G6

G6

G8. Carlshalton Theatre, 1991
High Street, Carshalton
BR: Carshalton
Access: public
Edward Cullinan Architects

This community and amateur theatre's largesse is cultural and professional rather than physical, but this might just be the real thing: thick architecture, worth travelling out to south London to see.

The scheme consists of two blocks: the 180 seat theatre fronting the street with an (adapted) existing facade; and an entirely new workshop block to the rear. The scheme deploys its fundamental architectural features so as to create presence, statement, and self-advertisement, lifting the High Street architecturally whilst proclaiming its cultural and communal ambitions. In the words of the architects, the conversion 'illustrates for us a way of building on the past, without imitating it, opening up and transforming an old shell and building afresh with the spirit and materials of our time'.

The 'spirit of our time' as seen by Cullinan and his practice might well begin with the admonition to stop philosophising about life and get used to it. The result is an architecture which is engaging rather than elitist, imbued with a contemporary equivalent of an Arts and Crafts sensibility, utilising ubiquitously available materials and readily accessible technologies to achieve its purposes and effects. The architecture is not only wrested from circumstances, but economically wrought from a constrained budget. It is a genuine small gem.

But it has fault (in our estimation): the rear workshop block, where the architectural quality thins out and a disparity between front and rear blocks is exposed. Otherwise, this is possibly among Cullinan's best work.

(Worth comparing with his Lambeth Centre and St Mary's at Barnes.)

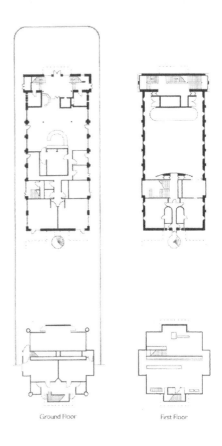

Ground Floor   First Floor

H. Transport architecture

H1. Waterloo International Terminal, 1993
Tube: Waterloo
Nicholas Grimshaw & Partners Ltd

H2. Stansted Airport, 1991
BR: Stansted (from Liverpool Street)
Sir Norman Foster & Partners

H3. East Croydon Station, 1992
BR (Croydon)
Alan Brookes Associates

H4. Redhill Station, 1990
BR (Near Reigate)
Troughton McAslan

H5. Tottenham Hale Station, 1991
BR, Tube
Alsop & Lyall

H6. Bridge Control Room, 1991
Isle of Dogs
Alsop and Lyall

H7. Docklands Light Railway stations, 1993
Isle of Dogs
Ahrends, Burton & Koralek

*Coherent transport planning (or lack of it) has
been one of the major planning issues of the
1980s. But, surprisingly, there are a number of
good examples to look at.*

*At the time of writing many projects are
in design or construction. This includes
Waterloo, but also a series of DLR stations in
Docklands by Ahrends Burton & Kolorek.
Stansted Airport (H2), we admit, stretches the
definition of London but, as its third airport and
as such a fine building, we consider that it is
reasonable to include (certainly inexcusable to
exclude). It is accessible from Liverpool Street
BR station.*

H1. Waterloo International Terminal

Access: public
At the time of going to press this building is
complete but unused. It is a remarkable piece of
design.

The principal feature of the scheme is a
400 metre long, sinuous roof structure
straddling the rail platforms. Beneath them are
the transfer facilities: concourses, ticket hall,
lounges, customs, shopping, car parking (at the
lowest level), etc. It is all very similar to what
one expects to find at an airport – apart from
such features as the refurbishment of existing
brick vaulting for back-up facilities.

The form of the roof structure
(engineered by YRM Anthony Hunt Associates)
had to accommodate a track layout provided by
British Rail – which, in turn, was constrained
by the tight site conditions. The western track
enjoys views of the Thames, prompting the
designers to provide large areas of glazing.
Their literally larger problem, however, was
how to enclose a variable shape with spans
between 35 and 50 m.

The arching is achieved with a three-pin
structure clearly articulated to express the
inherent forces (if you can interpret it). The
cladding was just as difficult, requiring a
pragmatic attitude that could reduce the
potential myriad of component sizes to
something reasonable. A loose fit system with
large overlaps and flexible gasketed joints does
the job of coping with the twisting geometry.

H2. Stansted Airport

Access: public

The overriding impressions given by Stansted airport is of urbanity, decisiveness and control. The architecture has a singular note which is powerful and effective: the huge spread-eagled structural trees which replicate themselves and arithmetically conjoin to form a powerful, sheltering architectural image. As a facility it demonstrates an organisational virtuousity and sleight of hand which makes the complex appear simple and straightforward e.g. the way all traffic is taken through a direct flow-path, mainly on one level. Its architectural solutions appear natural and self-evident.

This is the Foster practice at its best. The offer may appear to be merely one idea, but what breathtaking effect it has! Stansted has the supercilious quality one associates with star glamour – something which is there when one gets out of the train from Liverpool Street and is insistently present throughout this people and luggage processing artefact until one climbs aboard the inevitable 747.

The strength of the architecture, however, is also its Achilles heel. When it comes to the staff who want to stick posters on walls, the travellers desiring to purchase the *Sun* as well as the *Financial Times*, the commercial content that offers hamburgers as well as croissants – impacts upon the building that can be tacky and just ordinarily human – then Foster's approach to making architecture presents difficulties. In cultural terms it is rather inflexible and domineering. One senses a pursuit of perfection as an end in itself – an ambition apparently informed by an implicit intolerance of plurality and difference. (Admittedly, the alternative might have been another Terminal Four.)

One can only hope that Foster's extraordinary design is robust enough to cope, that he will not suffer the discomfort which no doubt troubled the ghost of a similarly radical architect, Inigo Jones, upon discovering the Covent Garden market beneath his elitest and supremely confident church portico, and the ladies of the Turkish bath houses occupying his piazza. It's a tough life producing art.

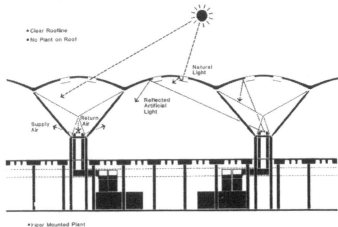

H3. East Croydon Station

Access: public

This is a classic example of the hi-tech approach to making buildings: an instrumental logic and concerns with constructional articulation are all important.

H3

The overriding feature of the station's *parti* is the employment of four tall masts from which hang two trusses providing 55m clear spans, thus fulfilling a characteristic hi-tech dream: the column-free space. Other fulfilled dreams at Croydon are transparency (lots of glass); minimal sections and profiles (more with less); custom-designed details (pushing the technological conversation); and maritime metaphors (the ramps to the platforms as gang-planks). At East Croydon, this is all handled with expertise and skill. The 10 million people who annually use the station now have something special to commute to and from each day.

H4. Redhill Station

Access: public

The principal feature of this station is the tall drum of its ticket hall – clearly a quotation from the work of Charles Holden (e.g. Arnos Grove underground station). Its glazed facade, white steelwork and dramatic overhang make a striking image, particularly at night. The drum grows sideways out of a single-storey base building with offices, toilets, etc., which also acts as the structural brace to the drum.

The platform has a long, entirely glazed waiting room articulated quite separately from the structure of the platform canopy overhead.

H4

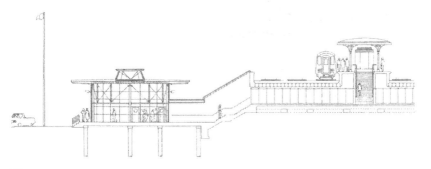

H4

H5. Tottenham Hale Station
Access: public
This station facilitates a link between the
underground system (Victoria Line) and the BR
Liverpool Street – Stansted trains. In the
architect's words, 'Architecturally, the station is
a clean and pure composition of white-painted
steelwork, transparent glass walls and silver
aluminium roof sheeting'. Alongside one of the
platforms is a dramatically curved building
housing the waiting room, a buffet, shop,
toilets, etc. The painted freizes are by Bruce
McLean.

H5

H6. Bridge Control Room
Access: private
This small project by Alsop and Lyall sits just
to the north of the Canary Wharf's first phase
(the part completed). It is primarily an
engineering project, but Alsop and Stormer's
input is quite evident. The bridge comprises a
pair of bascule lifting bridges, together with a
hydraulic plant building and control room. The
latter struts out from a structure housing the
plant, reaching up to the road level on the
bridge above. Its aesthetic is very Otto Wagner
(the telegraph office) – heavy steel, segmental
and chamfering plates, painted silver. Every
component and junction is exaggerated for
sculptural effect.

H5

H6

H7. Docklands Light Railway stations
Access: public
These stations are beyond the Isle of Dogs,
although Poplar is in that area. A 'kit of parts'
strategy has been employed to cope with the
different site conditions and an effort has been
made to integrate the designs with their
developmental context – a new and welcome
policy departure for the LDDC, even if it is a bit
late in the day.

H7

Index of architects

Aalto, Alvar   8, 26, 44, 47, 75, 104, 114
Ahrends Burton and Koralek   87, 109, 119, 122
Allies & Morrison   35, 59, 76
Allsopp, Kit Architects   17
Alsop & Lyall   119, 122
Alsop & Stormer   39, 119
Arad, Ron Associates   83, 84
Armstrong, Ken & Associates   112
Arup Associates   xii, 4–5, 100, 101, 112
Baker, Sir Herbert   1
BDP   20–21, 69
Belcher, J & J   1
Behnisch, Gunter   viii
Bergstrom, Lennart   98
Birkets & Associates   5
Bonnington, John Partnership   38
Branson Coates   59, 61
Brookes, Alan Associates   119, 121
Bunshaft, Gordon   75
Calatrava, Santiago   5
Campbell Zogolovitch Wilkinson & Gough
   (CZWG), viii, 20, 33, 37, 39, 59
Casson Conder Partnership   11, 53
Chamberlin Powell & Bond   13, 53
Chareau, Pierre   3, 81, 103
Chassay Architects   26, 85, 90
Chassay Wright   77, 83
Chipperfield, David Architects   81, 108
Colquhoun and Miller   8, 42
Conran Roche Architects   30, 33, 35, 36
Cooper, Sir Edwin   1
CTS - Douglas Clelland & Gavin Rae   87, 89
Cullinan, Edward Architects   95, 97, 104,
   110, 113, 116, 118
Cullum, Hugh & Nightingale, Richard   87, 89
Dance, George the Elder   1
Darbourne & Darke   54
Darke, Geoffrey   103
DEGW – Duffy Eley Griffone Worthington   2,
   77, 78, 101
Dixon, Jeremy & Fenella   xiv, 55–6, 69, 70
Dixon, Jeremy + BDP   20, 69
Ellwood, Craig   104
Erith & Terry   64, 105
Erskine, Ralph   77, 95, 98
Farrell, Terry and Company   viii, xv, 6, 9, 28,
   31, 46, 49, 58, 79, 80
Fitch RS   78
Foggo, Peter   4

Foster, Sir Norman Associates   xi, xiii, 48, 74,
   100, 102, 106, 114, 119, 120
Fowler, Vivien & Jestico, Tom   108
Fretton, Tony Architects   66
GMW Partnership   10
Gehry, Frank   43, 68, 112
Gilbert Scott, Sir George   75
Goff, Bruce   84
Goodhart-Rendel, HS   106
Gordon, Max   viii, xi, 48, 68
Gough, Piers   xiii
Grimshaw, Nicholas & Partners   viii, xiv, 7,
   24, 80, 95, 107, 110, 119
Gropius, Walter   35
Guimard, Hector   5
Hawksmoor, Nicholas   28, 31, 53
Herron Associates   51
Heysham, Terence   2
Holabird and Root   58
Holden, Charles   121
Hopkins, Michael and Partners   viii, 7, 36, 50,
   65, 66, 104
Horne, Trevor Architects   67
Hunt, Tony   5
Jestico + Whiles   50, 83
Jiricna , Eva Architects   60, 62
Johnson, Philip   5, 88
Jones, Horace   2
Jones, Inigo   46, 70, 120
Keats, Elana & Associates   13
Kjaer Richter   40
Koetter Kim Associates   19
Kohn Pederson Fox Associates   18
Lacey, Nicholas Jobst & Hyett   xiv, 17, 57
Lasdun, Sir Denys & Peter Softley &
   Associates   13
Ledoux, C-N   46
Levitt Bernstein Associates Ltd.   20
Lewerentz, Sigurd   44
Loos, Adolf   52
Lubetkin & Tecton   85, 90
Lutyens, Sir Edwin   1, 54
Lyall, John Architects   122
MacCormac Jamieson Prichard   30, 44, 110,
   117
Mather, Rick Architects   32, 60, 71, 85
Miller, John Partners   52, 55–6
Munkenbeck and Marshall   71
Nash, John   21, 64, 94, 100

Olbrich, Josef   52
Olins, Hanna   18–19
Outram, John Associates   viii, xiv, 22, 23
Patel, Pankaj and Taylor, Andrew   41, 42,116
Parry, Eric Associates   100, 103
Pei Cobb Freed & Partners   18–19
Pelli, Cesar & Associates   18–19
Perkins & Will   19
Penoyre & Prasad Architects   41, 116
Pollard Thomas & Edwards   33
Portman, John   107
Powell Partnership Moya   53, 54
Powell-Tuck, Connor & Orefelt   95, 99, 114
Reid, Richard Architects   40, 93
Rendel Palmer & Tritton   27
Rennie, John   31
Richardson, Sir Albert   7
Richardson, H H   5
Richmond, David & Partners   115
Rietveld, Gerrit   71
Ritchie, Ian Architects   29, 102
Rock Townsend   43, 77, 83, 84, 105
Rogers, Richard Partnership   viii, x, xii, xiv,
     2–3, 12, 22, 23, 25, 58, 96, 107
Rolfe Judd Partnership   10
Ronalds, Tim Architects   92
Rossi, Aldo   19
St John Wilson, Colin & Partners Ltd.   44, 75
Schinkel, K.F.   31
Shaw, Norman   54
Shepheard Epstein & Hunter   39

Sheppard Robson   32, 47
Smirke, Sidney   112
Soane, Sir John   1, 47, 48, 56, 94
SOM – Skidmore Owings & Merrill   viii, xii,
     4–5, 11, 18–19, 43, 100, 103
Spence, Robin   108
Squire, Michael Associates   33
Stanton Williams   28, 35, 61, 62
Stephen, Douglas & Partners   90
Stirling Wilford and Associates   viii, xi, 55–6,
     93
Tite, Sir William   1
Terry, Quinlan   viii, xiv, 63, 64
Townsend, Harrison   8
Troughton McAslan   18–19, 100, 102, 119,
     121
Twigg, Michael Brown & Partners   38
van Heyningen and Haward   87, 88
Venturi Rauch, Scott Brown & Associates   xi,
     47, 49, 56, 107
Wagner, Otto   9, 10, 122
Whitfield & Partners   54
Wickham Asscociates   33, 34, 91
Wild, David   82
Wilford, Michael   viii, xi
Wilkins, William   47
Wilson, Peter   87, 88
Winter, John and Associates   xii, 13, 87
Wolton, Georgie   108
Wright, Frank Lloyd   58, 114
Young, John   xiv

Index of buildings

Agar Road Studios **81**
Alban Gate **6**
Anchor Brewhouse 33
Anchorage, The 20
Arena, The **101**
Ark, The xiv, 70, 77, 95, 97, **98**
Ashland Place 76
Ashmill Street housing **69**
Bank of England 1
Barbican Centre 13
Battersea Church Road house 114
Bedfont Lakes xv, 7, 95, **104**
Billingsgate Securities Market **12**
Bisterne Avenue apartments 34, **91**
Blackburn house **88**
Bracken House **7**, 50, 61, 104
Bricklayer's Arms **115**
Bridge Control Room, Isle of Dogs 119, **122**
Bridge Wharf **77**
British Library 72, **75**
Broadgate Complex viii, xii, **4**, 34, 105
Bruges Place 77, **83**
Burlington Gardens jewellery shop 61
Burton house **87**
Butler's Wharf xiii, **33**, 38
Cabot Square Nos. 1, 10, 25, 20, 30 19
Canada Place No 1 19
Canary Wharf viii, xii, xiii, xiv, **18**
Carshalton Theatre xv, 110, **118**
Cascades xiv, **20**
Channel Four 58
China Wharf **37**
Chiswick Villa 88
Chomley Wood Garden Centre 92
Church Crescent housing 42
Circle, The **37**
Classic FM radio station 61
Clifton Nursery 69, **70**
Clore Gallery viii, xi, xiv, **55**
Clove Building 35, 76
Compass Point xiv, **21**, 29, 69
Comyn Ching 9, **49**
Corney & Barrow 34
Cornhill offices **10**, 62
Coutts Crescent **90**
Crowndale Centre 43, **84**, 93
Crown Reach **57**
Design Museum xiii, **35**
Docklands Light Railway **122**
Doctor's surgery **116**

Dufours Place 64
East Croydon Station **121**
Embankment Place **46**
Epping Town Hall xv, **93**
Equipment 62
Exchange House 5
Fenchurch Street offices **9**
Ferry Street housing **20**
Financial Times Printing Works xiv, 7, **24**
Finland Quay West **40**
Fleet Place viii, **11**
Foster offices **114**
Fowler/Jestico house **108**
Girozentrale Vienna **10**
Greenland Dock Control Building 39
Grimaldi Park House **76**, 77
Greenland Passage **40**
Hays Galleria 33, **38**
Highgate Group Practice **90**
Highpoint 85, 90
Hopkins office **66**
Heron Quays xiii, xiv, **17**, 39, 57
Homebase 24, 95, **107**
Horselydown development **34**
IBM Bedfont Lakes **104**
IBM Lodge Road **65**
Imagination **51**
Imperial War Museum xv, **112**
Imperial War Museum Shop 112
Informatics Teaching Laboratory 44
Insignia House **13**
Isle of Dogs Neigbourhood Centre **26**
Issey Miyake **62**
ITN 13, **74**
Jacksons Lane Theatre 92
Jazz Café **83**
Jigsaw, Brompton Road **61**
Jigsaw, Kensington High Street 61
Joe's Café **62**
Joseph **62**
Katherine Hamnett 61
Kensal Road warehouse 23
Kensington Place restaurant 34
Kenzo 61, 62
Knight house **108**
Kurskaya Station 46
Kriston Laundry 61
Lakes, The **39**
La Lumiere **32**
Lambeth Community Care Centre xv, **113**, 118
Lanark Road housing 21, **70**
Lancaster Road offices **71**

Lauriston Studios   **42**
Le Champenois   34
Legends   **60**
Lewis, John department store   95, **109**
Leyton Fire Station   **43**
Lillington Gardens   54
Lisson/Bell Street galleries   **66**
Lisson Grove offices   66, **67**
Lloyd's of London   x, xi, **2**, 5, 25
London Bridge City   14
London Wall, no. 85   **11**, 54
M25 motorway   xv
Ma & Pa   60
Mellor, David building   33, **36**
Metropolis Studios   95, **99**
Metropolitan Police Office   54
Michelin building   62
Milton Gate   **13**
Minster Court   **10**
More, Thomas Complex   32
Mound Stand, Lord's Cricket Ground   xiv, **65**
New Concordia Wharf   33, 38
New Crane Wharf   30
New Square   104
Nightingale house   **89**
North Colonnade   19
Now and Zen   **60**
One Off Studio   **84**
Pelican Wharf   30
Porters North   **78**
Porters South   **78**
Poultry No 1   1
Queen Elizabeth II Conference Centre   11, **53**, 54
Queen Mary & Westfield College library and student accommodation   **44**
Queen Street offices   **9**
Rayleigh Gardens Surgery   116
Redhill Station   **121**
Regent's Park villas   xiv, **64**
Regent's Wharf   **77**
Reuters Technical Services Centre   xiv, **25**, 74
Richmond House   **54**
Richmond Riverside   64, **105**
Rochester Place houses   **82**
Roy Square   **29**
Royal College of Art (RCA)   52
Royal Victoria Dock Pumping Station   **23**
Saatchi Gallery   viii, xi, 48, **68**
Sackler Gallery   viii, xi, **48**, 55

Saffron Wharf   33, **36**
Sainsbury Centre   xv, 106
Sainsbury supermarket and housing   xiv, 7, 24, **80**
Sainsbury Wing, National Gallery   viii, xi, **47**, 55
Shadwell Basin   **30**
South Bank Arts Centre   46
St Katharine's Dock   xii, 30
St George in the East   31
St Mark's Road housing   21, **69**, 70, 117
St Mary's Church, Barnes   **97**, 118
Stansted Airport   xv, **120**
Stephen Bull Restaurant   **59**, 76
Sterling Hilton Hotel   xv, **106**
Stevens building   **52**
Stewart Street Pumping Station   **23**
Stockley Park:
A1, A1.2, A2.1, A2.3, A3.1, A1.3, A2.2, A3.2, B1, B5, B7, The Arena   xv, **101**
Stockley Park - B2/B4, B3, B8   **102**
Stockley Park - W3   **103**
Strathleven & Mauleverer Road housing   **117**
Stukeley Place   **50**
Tate Gallery   xi, **55**
Tate restaurants and bookshop   55, **56**
Thames Flood Barrier   xv, **27**
Thames Wharf Studios   95, **96**
Thames Wharf apartments   **96**
Tobacco Dock   28, **31**
Tottenham Hale Station   **122**
TV-AM   xiv, **79**
van Heyningen/Haward House   **88**
Vauxhall Cross   xiv, **58**
Vining Street housing   xiv, **117**
Vogan Mills   33
Walthamstow Coroner's Court   **92**
Waterloo International Terminal   **119**
Water sports centre   17
Weinreb House   **89**
West Ferry Circus nos. 1 & 7   19
Whistler Restaurant   **55**
Whistles   **61**
Whitechapel Gallery   **8**, 56
Whittington Day Care Centre   110, 113
Wild, David houses   **82**
Wilson & Gough   **62**
Wolfe Crescent   **39**
Zen Central   60

Photographic credits

The authors would like to thank Marlies Hentrup for the photograph of Jim Stirling and also the following people who have kindly supplied photographs for this publication.

Alban Gate – Martin Charles
Ark, The – Timothy Soar
Bell Street Gallery – Martin Charles
Billingsgate Securities Market – Eamonn O'Mahony
Bishopsgate – Wordsearch/Alan Williams
Bracken House – Martin Charles
Bricklayer's Arms – Jo Reid & John Peck
Bridge Control Room – Alsop & Stormer
Bridge Wharf – Ken Allinson
Bruges Place – Matthew Weinreb
Burton house – John Donat
Canary Wharf – Olympia & York
Canary Wharf buildings – Ken Allinson
Canary Wharf tower – Ken Allinson
Carshalton Theatre – Dennis Gilbert
Cascades – Jo Reid & John Peck
China Wharf – Jo Reid & John Peck
Circle, The – Jordi Sarra
Clifton Nurseries – Jo Reid & John Peck
Clore Gallery – Graham Challifour
Compass Point – Jo Reid & John Peck
Comyn Ching Triangle – Richard Bryant
Cornhill 62–64 – Ken Allinson
Crowndale Centre – Ken Allinson
Crown Reach – Carlo Roberti
Doctor's surgery – Dennis Gilbert
East Croydon Station – John Linden
Embankment Place – Nigel Young
Financial Times Printing Works – Jo Reid & John Peck
Finland Quay West – Dennis Gilbert
Fleet Place – Alan Williams/Wordsearch
Foster offices – Richard Davies
Fowler/Jestico house – Jo Reid & John Peck
Girozentrale Vienna – Martin Charles
Greenland Passage – Martin Charles
Grimaldi Park House – Peter Cook
Highgate Group Practice – Douglas Stephens & Partners
Heron Quays – Martin Charles
Homebase – Jo Reid & John Peck
Imperial War Museum – Nicholas Gentilli & Associates

Isle of Dogs Neighbourhood Centre – Tait's Gallery
Issey Miyake – Stanton Williams
ITN – Richard Davies
Jazz Café – Steve Reynolds
Joe's Café – Alistair Hunter
Joseph – Peter Cook
La Lumiere – Dennis Gilbert
Lambeth Community Care Centre – Ken Allinson
Lancaster Road offices – Denis Gilbert
Lauriston Studios – Rupert Truman
Legends – Alistair Hunter
Lewis. John department store – Martin Charles
Leyton Fire Station – Morley von Sternberg
Lisson Gallery – Martin Charles
Lisson Grove offices – Trevor Horne
Lloyd's of London – Peter Cook
London Wall, no. 85 – Casson Conder
Mellor, David building – Peter Cook
Metropolis Studios – Richard Davies
Midland Bank – Jo Reid & John Peck
Milton Gate – Phil Sayer
Mound Stand, Lord's Cricket Ground – Richard Bryant
Nightingale house – Charlotte Wood
One Off Studio – Keith Collie
Porters South – Chris Gascoigne
Queen Elizabeth II Conference Centre – Matthew Weinreb
Queen Mary & Westfield College library – Martin Charles
Queen Mary & Westfield College student accommodation – Peter Cook
Redhill Station – Peter Cook
Regent's Park villas – Nick Carter
Regent's Wharf – Morley von Sternberg
Reuters Technical Services Centre – Ken Allinson
Richmond House – Jeremy Cockayne
Richmond Riverside – Claude Mercier
Roy Square – Ian Ritchie
Royal Victoria Dock Pumping Station – Matthew Antrobus
Saatchi Gallery – Dorothy Saatchi
Sackler Gallery – Dennis Gilbert
Sainsbury housing – Jo Reid & John Peck
Sainsbury supermarket – Jo Reid & John Peck
Sainsbury Wing, National Gallery – Matt Wargo
Shadwell Basin – Martin Charles

St Mary's Church Barnes – Martin Charles
Stansted Airport – Ken Kirkwood
Stephen Bull Restaurant – Peter Cook
Stevens building – Martin Charles
Stewart Street Pumping Station – John Outram
Stirling Hilton Hotel – Manser Associates
Stockley Park (B3) – Richard Davies
Stockley Park (B2/B4) – Peter Cook
Strathleven and Mauleverer Road Housing – Simon Warren
Stukeley Place – Jo Reid & John Peck
Tate Coffee Shop – Dixon Jones
Tate Bookshop – Martin Charles
Thames Flood Barrier – Business Development Unit Library

Thames Wharf Studios – Mateo Piazzo
Thames Wharf apartments – Mateo Piazzo
Tobacco Dock – Richard Bryant
TV-AM – Richard Bryant
van Heyningen/Haward House – Birkin Haward
Vauxhall Cross – Nigel Young
Vining Street – Simon Doling
Walthamstow Coroner's Court – Charlotte Wood
Waterloo International Terminal – Michael Dyer Associates
Weinreb House – Matthew Weinreb
Whitechapel Gallery – Martin Charles
Wolfe Crescent – Jo Reid & John Peck

Made in the USA
Las Vegas, NV
04 February 2022